"Looking for a self-help guide for cravings tha[...] further than this book. There are many self-help books out there, but very few are evidenced-based and written by clinical psychologists and professors in psychology such as are these two authors. Based on these underpinnings of original research and clinical practice, these two authors compassionately guide you step by step to changing your relationship to cravings."

—**JoAnne Dahl, PhD**, professor emerita in the department of psychology at Uppsala University in Sweden, licensed psychologist, psychotherapist, peer-reviewed acceptance and commitment therapy (ACT) trainer, and Association for Contextual Behavioral Science (ACBS) fellow

"Written by two leading scholars in ACT, this book brings together decades of research and clinical practice on how to cope with cravings and break addictive patterns. It's an excellent guide for learning how to develop a new relationship with your cravings so they don't push you around so much, with a wealth of practical tips and skills that apply to a wide range of craving-related problems."

—**Michael Levin, PhD**, professor at Utah State University, and coauthor of *Innovations in Acceptance and Commitment Therapy*

"*Cravings and Addictions* is an excellently crafted, interactive book with touching personal stories of the authors' own struggles with cravings leading into innovative exercises that use cutting-edge theory from psychological science. We all struggle with certain cravings and addictions to varying degrees. *Cravings and Addictions* provides key tips on how to surf the cravings, urges, impulses, and desires that underpin whatever habit it is that you want to break."

—**Louise McHugh**, professor in the school of psychology at University College Dublin; peer-reviewed ACT trainer; author of more than one hundred academic papers in the area of ACT and relational frame theory (RFT); and coauthor of *The Self and Perspective Taking*

"If you want to stop fighting with cravings and instead live life more fully, this book will show you the way. Honest, insightful, and full of clinical wisdom, the authors masterfully show you steps you can take to overcome your struggles. Using case studies combined with expert commentary, it is an excellent resource for anyone wanting to transform their struggle with cravings or therapists wanting to learn this approach."

—**Andrew Gloster**, professor of psychology, head of division
of clinical psychology and intervention science, and head of
postgraduate training in process-based psychotherapy
at University of Basel

"This book is a highly engaging, user-friendly application of ACT for individuals who are struggling with the use of substances, including food. The authors masterfully balance instruction with compassion in a way that creates a setting for empowerment and change, and readers will easily relate to the client examples. The intense focus on cravings is novel, making this a must-read for lay persons and professionals alike."

—**Angela L. Stotts, PhD**, professor and vice chair for research
at the UTHealth McGovern Medical School at the University
of Texas Health Science Center at Houston

"I found this book so helpful—both informative and easily applicable. In fact, I received bad news while reading it, experienced a food craving, and was able to manage it effectively using the tools the authors provided! I loved the blend of classic and new ACT exercises along with the relatable case examples. Anyone who struggles with cravings of any sort should read this book!"

—**Jill Stoddard, PhD**, author of *Be Mighty*, and coauthor of
The Big Book of ACT Metaphors

"Just about everyone craves something. But as we give in to our cravings, they often grow in size and strength, and can quite literally take over our lives. But it doesn't have to be that way. This gentle and compassionate book offers you a newer, science-backed approach to help you break the cycle of cravings and additions so you can reclaim your power and your life. If you work with this book, you'll find that you may have cravings, but they no longer control you. Instead, you gain the space and freedom to do what you truly care about, cravings or not."

—**John P. Forsyth, PhD**, professor of psychology and director of the Anxiety Disorders Research Program at the University at Albany, and coauthor of *The Mindfulness and Acceptance Workbook for Anxiety* and *Anxiety Happens*

"This book is powerful. It unpacks the myths about cravings, and helps you understand your physical, social, habitual, and emotional coping strategies. It puts the reader back in charge by helping them with strategies for success that comprise good behavioral science plus human warmth via kindness and compassion. You will feel your motivation rise as you discover your trade-off. Living inside your immediate craving vs. valued living and being healthier, happier, having more money, better relationships, and greater confidence. This book is clear and easy to follow. If you want to change your life, I thoroughly recommend it."

—**Louise Hayes, PhD**, clinical psychologist, and coauthor of *The Thriving Adolescent*; *Your Life, Your Way*; and *Get Out of Your Mind and Into Your Life for Teens*

CRAVINGS AND ADDICTIONS

Free Yourself from the **Struggle**
of **Addictive Behavior** with
Acceptance and **Commitment Therapy**

Maria Karekla, PhD | Megan M. Kelly, PhD

New Harbinger Publications, Inc.

Publisher's Note

Distributed in Canada by Raincoast Books

NEW HARBINGER PUBLICATIONS is a registered trademark of
New Harbinger Publications, Inc.

Copyright © 2021 by Maria Karekla, Megan Kelly
           New Harbinger Publications, Inc.
           5674 Shattuck Avenue
           Oakland, CA 94609
           www.newharbinger.com

Cover design by Amy Daniel

Acquired by Elizabeth Hollis Hansen

Edited by Kristi Hein

All Rights Reserved

Library of Congress Cataloging-in-Publication Data

Names: Karekla, Maria, author. | Kelly, Megan (Megan M.), author.
Title: Cravings and addictions : free yourself from the struggle of addictive behavior with
    acceptance and commitment therapy / Maria Karekla, PhD, Megan Kelly, PhD.
Description: Oakland, CA : New Harbinger Publications, [2022] | Includes bibliographi-
    cal references.
Identifiers: LCCN 2021033401 | ISBN 9781684038336 (trade paperback)
Subjects: LCSH: Substance abuse--Treatment. | Acceptance and commitment therapy.
Classification: LCC RC564 .K375 2022 | DDC 362.29--dc23
LC record available at https://lccn.loc.gov/2021033401

Printed in the United States of America

23   22   21

10   9   8   7   6   5   4   3   2   1   First Printing

Maria

To my family, who cultivate in me the most coveted craving of all—to live and to love.

To my coauthor, my cherished friend and cheerleader. To my clients, who allow me to touch their lives, hopefully for the better.

Megan

To my family, who have always believed in me and what I value. To my coauthor, for her many years of close friendship and support. To the veterans I have worked with, who are the embodiment of committed action.

Contents

Foreword   vii

Introduction   1

1   Understanding Cravings   8

2   Why Should We Give Up or Continue Addictions?   20

3   Why Manage Craving and Change Addictive Behaviors?   30

4   Controlling Cravings Doesn't Work   44

5   Willingness to Make Room for Cravings   56

6   Taking a Step Back from Your Cravings   66

7   Separating Ourselves from Cravings   78

8   Mindfulness: Taming the Craving Horse   89

9   Making Friends with Ourselves: Self-Compassion as the Antidote to Self-Stigma   108

10   Having Your Cravings and Living Too   122

11   Dealing with Obstacles to Managing Cravings   136

12   Getting Support for Managing Cravings   149

13   Managing Cravings for the Long Run   167

Conclusion   179

Acknowledgments   183

References   185

Foreword

The great author, Mark Twain, famously said: "Giving up smoking is easy...I've done it hundreds of times." This witty line speaks to an important truth: breaking "bad habits" is not easy—especially when that habit is so deeply entrenched, so powerful and pervasive, that we label it as an addiction. Twain also said, "Habit is habit and not to be flung out of the window by any man, but coaxed downstairs a step at a time." And that is precisely what the authors of this book will help you to do, using the science-based approach of acceptance and commitment therapy (ACT).

ACT is a powerful model for changing behavior, with over three thousand published studies showing its effectiveness. Step-by-step this book takes you gently and compassionately through the ACT approach, teaching you all the skills you'll need to stop struggling with addictions and start living a richer, fuller life. Whether it's an addiction to drugs, alcohol, cigarettes, junk food, or anything else you can think of, there's a small set of simple but powerful tools that can help you to overcome the cravings, urges, impulses, and desires that underpin your "habit." Within these pages, psychologists Maria Karekla and Megan Kelly, both ACT experts, will take you through these tools and show you how to effectively apply them.

You may be surprised at much of what you learn within this book. Many of the tools and strategies are counterintuitive; they go against the conventional wisdom. They are radically different to popular "common-sense" approaches such as positive thinking, distraction, or trying to "resist your urges." But novel as they are, these methods are based on a firm foundation of solid scientific research. So, bring along an attitude of openness and curiosity; a willingness to experiment, and try out new things.

As you play around with your new ACT skills, you're sure to find, like millions of other people, that they have a huge, positive impact on your life. You'll discover how to take the power out of your cravings, so they no longer jerk you around. And better ways to handle the problems in your life, and all those painful thoughts and feelings that go with them. And most importantly of all, how to build a more satisfying and fulfilling life, while being the sort of person you truly want to be.

So good luck for the journey ahead. I encourage you to make the most of the great wisdom and compassion of your two excellent guides.

All the best,

Russ Harris

Introduction

Are you struggling to break free from a problematic addiction—for example, to smoking, drinking alcohol, taking drugs, overeating? Are you subject to persistent cravings that pull you back into addictive behaviors you want to leave behind? Have you tried everything you can think of to stop having or giving in to cravings, but find they keep coming back stronger than ever? You are not alone!

As clinicians, we've worked for a combined total of over forty years with clients whose addictive use of substances like alcohol, drugs, tobacco, or food has kept them stuck, feeling helpless, in life patterns that are unsatisfying, saddening, or even destructive. Our clients have found the most success with stopping the addictive behaviors and living the lives they want when they can effectively conquer their cravings. In this book, we will help you understand and effectively manage your cravings so you can live the life you want.

What Are Cravings?

Cravings are intense desires for using or consuming certain substances with the goal of feeling pleasure and satisfaction. (Though the word is used more broadly to mean strong desires for experiences, possessions, or even people, for the purposes of this book cravings are desires for any type of consumable substance.) Cravings are a key component of addiction-related problems, including addictions to substances like tobacco, alcohol, and drugs. They also contribute to the obesity epidemic because they are associated with our intense desire for certain foods that often aren't healthy for us (particularly those high in carbohydrates, sugars, salts, and fats).

Cravings are a common problem for people with addictions, and many struggle to manage them. It is no surprise that most of us report having cravings. Research finds that cravings are reported by 58 to 97 percent of the general population (Gendall, Joyce, & Sullivan, 1997), occurring as often as two to four times per week (Hill, 2007). Despite their high prevalence, we often experience cravings as unwanted, something that we *must not* have, and substantial obstacles to overcoming addictions. We struggle to manage or resist them.

Most of us who deal with addictive behaviors know the dire consequences of our behaviors, including the steep price often paid in terms of our health and relationships. However, many of us still struggle to manage, limit, or stop cravings related to our addictive behaviors. Many of these behaviors and associated cravings are as much a psychological as a physical addiction. We will explore this more in chapter 1. But as hard as it is to curb addictive behaviors, you can do this! There are effective ways of tackling our physical and psychological need for these substances that we desire so much—ways not based on the assumption that we need to completely change what we want, what we like, and how we live.

The Problem with Old Solutions

Many approaches to managing cravings and addictions share two problematic and false assumptions:

- We must rid ourselves of cravings to become "addiction-free."

- We must avoid anything that ever causes us to crave.

These two nearly impossible goals set us up for failure. First, as we've noted, cravings are normal and unavoidable. Common events—anything and everything—can trigger a craving. Trying to avoid them is so difficult it only gets us more stuck.

In this book we take a different approach. We affirm that, to make an important life change, we need to change not whether we *experience* cravings, but whether we can *change our relationship to* and perceptions of cravings and addictions. This doesn't demand some kind of perfection, or that we structure our lives to avoid temptation. It's actually achievable.

Many people deal with several types of cravings; for example, smoking, eating, drinking, and using drugs. Approaching each separately doesn't make a whole lot of sense, and it can be exhausting trying to manage them all at the same time! But we often need help to learn how to manage several different cravings at once.

Fortunately, the principles and practices we'll teach you here can help you break free from the grip of cravings, even when these are frequent or for several types of substances. You'll do this not by abolishing cravings (a superhuman feat) but by learning to change how you deal with them and to focus on the important things you want from life.

Choosing a Values-Based Life

Many who struggle with addictive patterns know the serenity prayer, which asks for "the serenity to accept things I can't change, courage to change the things I can, and wisdom to know the difference." It is an inspiring expression of what a life without substance use might look like. And many admirers wonder *How? How can I accept the unchangeable and change the unacceptable?*

In this book we'll teach you to put the serenity creed into action, particularly in relation to managing cravings and addictions, using tools drawn from an approach you may not have heard of. Acceptance and commitment therapy (ACT: read as one word, "act") is a values-based approach for managing a wide range of psychological problems, including addictions. Based on cutting-edge research into how the human mind works, ACT is a clinically proven successful treatment. ACT has a strong research base for improving conditions in which cravings are a central reason for addictions starting and continuing. For over thirty years, ACT practitioners have created perspectives, practices, skills, and tools that allow people to choose to live each day according to their values rather than according to habits or compulsions.

ACT is named for two key themes: learning how to *accept* those things that are out of your control and *commit* to changing those things you can change to make your life better. *Cravings and Addictions* is less about making cravings go away and more about freeing you from the struggle involved in trying to make them go away. Freed from this unwinnable struggle, you are better able to make positive life choices, whether the cravings are there or not. You can move in a direction that is important to you. Using an ACT approach, we will help you actively learn new skills to manage cravings and improve your life.

The principles of ACT (the therapeutic approach) can be summarized using the same acronym: Accept, Choose a Direction, and Take Action.

Accept

Imagine playing with one of those finger traps where you slip one index finger into each end of a tube, then try to pull them out. That seems like the obvious solution. But with pulling, the tube just tightens on your fingers. Your mind tells you to pull harder, with more strength and will. But it doesn't work! The squeezing on your fingers reduces circulation, which starts to hurt. The harder you try to pull out of the trap, the more stuck you become.

Interestingly, the solution is to do just the opposite: to move your fingers *into* the finger trap instead. Suddenly the tube loosens and you can get your fingers out! By leaning in, you created space in the tube, and freedom to move. This is *acceptance*.

Cravings work in a similar way. Our instinctive solution (and the solution that's reinforced in our culture) is to try to pull away from them. But if you do this, you tend to get mentally trapped inside the struggle with the craving, such that it can seem like giving in to it is the only way to ease the struggle. This of course leads to more problems and discomfort. With acceptance practices, you learn to lean into the discomfort of managing cravings. You acknowledge craving and make room for it in your life. Rather than staying trapped in a battle with your cravings, acceptance gives you enough room to move around and live your life.

Choose a Direction

Have you ever attempted to visit a new place and come to a crossroad in your path? Which direction is the right one to take to get you where you want to go? Each time a craving shows up it's like reaching a crossroad. Effectively dealing with cravings means deciding which road to take.

When you create space by accepting cravings and their associated thoughts and feelings, it becomes more possible to choose your path and create a rich, full, and meaningful life. To do that, you'll need to spend some time exploring what's important and meaningful to you, deep in your heart. *Values* are your heart's deepest desires for what you want to do and how you want to be. ACT has powerful tools and techniques for clarifying values and orienting life around them.

Living a values-based life is a process—something that you will work on and be committed to now and over the course of your life. You'll find that the same is true of managing cravings. Managing cravings and living a valued life are not about crossing the finish line and you're done. They are part of a lifelong journey.

Take Action

Using your values as a guide and your own personal compass, you'll learn to set goals to (1) manage your cravings and (2) take action to change your life for the better. In the process, you'll continue to develop a sense of meaning, purpose, and vitality.

We are *not* saying that, once you read or work through this book, you will never have cravings again. Nor do we aim to help you get rid of the cravings. This is on purpose. Remember: cravings are a normal part of life. And you can have a rich and meaningful life even in the presence of cravings. Your cravings don't have to rule your life. Instead, when you live each day to its fullest, the struggle with cravings and other uncomfortable feelings that seemed so important and necessary no longer seems so important. The way you approach life is much different.

"Live each day to the fullest" sounds like a great slogan. But we're not here to sling slogans. This book emerges from our years of practical, skills-based work with our clients. We'll teach you how to stop fighting your cravings and other uncomfortable feelings and thoughts, reduce your suffering, and accomplish what is important to you.

An Important Note Before We Move On

While we strongly encourage you to seek out professional help for any addictive behavior (including problematic eating, and smoking), it is important to note that if you have an addiction to alcohol and drugs, you may need to go through a medical-detoxification program to stop using these substances safely. You may have developed a physical dependence on (that is, physical need for) alcohol and drugs, so you need more and more of the substances to obtain the original effect. If you abruptly stop using alcohol, opiates, or benzodiazepines, you may experience withdrawal symptoms. These withdrawal symptoms can be difficult to tolerate on their own. In some cases, attempting an at-home detoxification ("detox") can be dangerous. This is why we strongly encourage you to seek out professional medical help with this process. It is important to not go through detox alone—you will need help in your first few weeks of sobriety. Even for other drugs with less severe withdrawal symptoms, we strongly encourage you to seek out professional help and rehabilitation as well. In conjunction with professional help, this book can be a guide to help you learn how to deal more effectively with cravings in your recovery.

How to Use This Book

Each chapter teaches different components that can help you take effective ACTion toward managing cravings and, most important, creating the life you want. We'll use case examples from clients who have struggled with problems similar to yours, plus examples from situations in our own lives, noting who is speaking: Maria, Megan, or "we."

Each chapter includes metaphors and exercises to help you understand the concepts and, most important, practice. Take any learning from this book and try it out for yourself with your own cravings. Each chapter is independent as well as related to the rest, so you can start to apply each suggestion immediately—no need to wait until you finish the book. Many clients like to go back and forth with the ideas and concepts learned. As you discover what works for you, feel free to adapt and make this material your own. You'll find a wealth of online free tools at http://www.new harbinger.com/48336. We reference them throughout the book, but you can download them now if you like, and they'll be ready for later use.

We hope you find our approach useful; that you gain new knowledge and skills with every page; and that these enhance your life and well-being. Let's get started!

CHAPTER 1

Understanding Cravings

Amy   *For me, eating and anxiety went hand in hand. I had strong cravings to eat whenever I was anxious. When I had stress at work, I came home and reached for food to manage it. If I had a bad interaction with someone at work, I would eat to make myself feel better. I ate junk food to relax. But it wasn't making the stress go away. I wasn't managing my anxiety in a healthy way.*

Amy is describing the phenomenon of cravings—an experience you probably recognize. Since you're reading this book, it's likely you also struggle with cravings. You may have tried to control your cravings by avoiding situations that provoke cravings, limiting where you go and who you see. Maybe you've tried to distract yourself to buy time for the craving to pass, or tried to bury those cravings and ignore them. All this effort can be exhausting. And when it wears you down, you're vulnerable to giving in. Then you're left feeling depressed or angry or disappointed with yourself. The harder you try to control your cravings, the more you lose. It's like trying to play a rigged game.

There is another way!

As discussed in the introduction, we define cravings as a strong desire to use a substance or a particular type of food. Addictions are defined by the experience of a physical or psychological need for a habit-forming substance, like certain foods high in levels of salt, sugar, fat; cigarettes; alcohol; and some drugs. When addicted to a substance, we can experience cravings for it, or strong preoccupying thoughts about wanting to use it. Because cravings are a defining feature of addiction, the experience of cravings was included as a symptom of substance use disorders in the latest (fifth edition) *Diagnostic and Statistical Manual of Mental Disorders* (DSM-5).

Cravings often make it difficult for people to stop engaging in addictive behaviors; they are a prime reason for relapse. Thus we aim to give you and others, like Amy, tools to successfully manage cravings. Again, you won't learn how to banish cravings—that is not possible. Rather, the aim is to learn new ways to behave when they show up so you can live the life you want.

Why, When, How, and Where Cravings Occur

Cravings are our brain's programmed response to environmental cues. When these cues are connected to food, tobacco, drugs, and alcohol, addictions to them can develop over time, through biological, behavioral, psychological, social, and environmental factors like these:

- A family history of addiction
- Seeing others engaging in the addictive behavior
- Availability of what we crave
- Messages from advertising and media
- Sensation seeking (seeking out thrilling or exciting experiences)

There are four overarching factors that tend to lead to cravings for food, nicotine, and other substances:

- We develop a physical addiction to a substance over time.
- We use a substance often enough to develop a psychological habit (which can accompany physical addictions, but is not the same thing).
- We experience challenging emotions—anxiety, sadness, anger— and seek relief or comfort from the substance.
- We've used the substance often in response to social cues.

Let's look at how each type of factor might affect us.

Cravings May Accompany Physical Addiction

First, cravings often arise when we have a physical addiction to a substance. Substances such as tobacco, alcohol, drugs, and food (particularly foods rich in fat and sugar) stimulate our bodies to release neurotransmitters. These chemical messengers create pleasurable feelings that act as teaching signals. One such neurotransmitter is *dopamine.* Dopamine plays a key role in the body's reward system, which helps us to think, plan, focus, and pursue things we find interesting and pleasurable. Dopamine is a critical component in the development of addictions, since it provides the pleasurable feeling we get when we use substances like certain foods, tobacco, alcohol, and drugs. Our brain links the substance (nicotine in a cigarette, alcohol in a drink) and the good feeling, and then the substance itself triggers a very strong desire—a craving—for more of the substance.

Over time, when we repeatedly use substances, they can actually change our brain structure and chemical composition. For instance, studies have shown strong evidence of brain activation when people who are addicted to food, cigarettes, alcohol, or drugs are shown pictures linked to these substances.

If we've taken the substance for a long time and developed a dependence, we may experience withdrawal symptoms—a variety of bodily sensations (flu-like symptoms, nausea, shaky hands), emotions (irritability, restlessness), and thoughts (*one cigarette is all I need right now*)—if we stop consuming it. These symptoms can range from mild to serious, depending on the substance and how long we have used it. Sometimes withdrawal can be dangerous without proper treatment and supervision. For instance, alcohol withdrawal may lead to seizures that can be dangerous, so medical intervention is important. Again, if you plan to stop using substances like alcohol or other drugs, we strongly advise you to discuss this process with your health care providers and develop a plan for doing this as safely as possible.

Because of this physical addiction, medications that block the effects of substances in the brain can be particularly helpful for managing cravings. For instance, medications like buprenorphine and methadone effectively reduce cravings for opiates. Tobacco-cessation medications like nicotine patches and lozenges can reduce the intensity of cravings and withdrawal symptoms. Sometimes people think they should have more willpower and tough it out (more on this shortly) without medical assistance. But by reducing the intensity of your cravings, these medications can improve your chances of learning how to better manage them. Again, we advise you to discuss with your health care providers options for ending your use of addictive substances.

However, we can also make the mistake of believing that medications are the only thing we need to manage cravings. Medications can play an important role in reducing the intensity of cravings, but cravings will still occur for other reasons, which we will explain. Therefore it is important to learn how to manage cravings with new coping tools and strategies rather than relying solely on medication.

Habitual Behaviors Lead to Cravings

People, places, and things become linked to the pleasurable feelings tied to neurotransmitters like dopamine. This process leads to cravings when our brain learns to associate those pleasurable feelings with situations in which we use substances. Such cravings occur frequently, particularly since we often eat food, smoke cigarettes, drink alcohol, and use drugs many times in a day.

How many times have you had chocolate over your lifetime? And in what situations have you had chocolate? We often have chocolate for dessert as a way of ending our meal. Now if you repeatedly have chocolate at the end of your meal, your mind starts to learn to expect chocolate at the end of the meal. That makes you more likely to think *I've finished dinner—time for chocolate!* And this situation causes you to crave chocolate.

Smokers often say, "Drinking coffee and having a cigarette go hand in hand." Once these are paired, the mind starts to associate coffee with having a cigarette. Then if you have a coffee *without* a cigarette, your mind starts to tell you that you *need* to have a cigarette with your coffee; you just won't feel right or get the same pleasure from drinking coffee without a cigarette. Your mind tells you that something is missing and that a cigarette will make it feel right.

These cravings can be hard to ignore or push away. We often give in to them because it takes too much effort to fight them. But we can change how we approach our habits and reduce the intensity of habit-related cravings over time. For instance, if you stop eating chocolate after dinner, over time the craving will eventually fade. You will not experience these cravings forever, particularly not as intensely. In this book, we'll teach you strategies for managing these cravings better so you're more prepared for dealing with them when they pop up in different situations.

Strong Emotions Spur Cravings

If you grew up watching old movies, you may have noticed that when a character was upset, stressed, or angry, they would reach for a smoke or have a drink. One way we learn about how to deal with our emotions is by watching others, listening to others' advice, or through our own trial and error. Somewhere in our history, we also learned to pair the use of specific substances or food with certain emotions. Thus we may often develop strong cravings when we feel stressed, anxious, angry, or depressed. After we use a substance, we feel immediate relief from the craving and link that with feeling less stressed and anxious. These are extremely common situations. When we feel stressed, we often reach for something comforting to eat, a cigarette, a drink, or recreational drugs. Emotions and thoughts can lead to very strong cravings. For a short time that relief feels good, but the cravings inevitably come back. And we reach for food, drugs, or cigarettes to feel better again. The cycle keeps repeating.

Sometimes cravings appear out of the blue, even if we haven't been using a substance for a long time. For instance, you may get bad news and then feel a strong craving for a drink, even if you haven't had alcohol for several years. For this reason, it is important to have a plan for these types of cravings. We will spend a lot of time focusing on these types of challenging triggers to help you feel better prepared for dealing with and overcoming them. There are very good ways of managing emotional cravings that can work for you!

Social Situations Cue Cravings

We often have cravings around other people, particularly people who use substances in front of us. Many of the substances associated with cravings are ones we may have used many times in social situations, such as when we go out to eat or hang out at a bar with our friends. We associate having fun with being around people we love or enjoy hanging out with, and what we do together may involve the use of a substance. So being around friends and family—or even the mention of the name of a person we would smoke with, go out for drinks with, share food with—is enough to bring on strong cravings.

If you're committed to not drinking, but you are at a party with friends and several of them are drinking, it can be hard to resist drinking with them. You may experience pressure to feel like everyone else and partake in using substances. You may not want to feel out of place when others are using. Drinking, smoking, or using drugs in the presence of others can also make you feel closer to people, like you have tighter social bonds. And using substances with others can be enjoyable. It can be hard to say no to cravings if someone offers you a cigarette or a drink. But there are ways to overcome these cravings as well.

EXERCISE: Your Craving Cues

Let's explore when cravings occur for you. Becoming aware of your cravings and understanding why they occur is the first step in the process of effectively managing your cravings and your life. It is the first step in developing your plan. The table here gives examples of common cravings. In a journal or notebook, write down each type of craving (physical, habitual, emotional, social) and list as many situations as you can think of where you have a strong craving for a substance. Or start by listing situations where cravings arise, then decide what type of craving goes with each situation. In the online free tools that accompany this book, you can find an empty table to start with.

Type of Craving	Situation
Physical	Wanting a cigarette when I haven't had one in an hour
Habitual	Wanting to eat chocolate after dinner
Social	Wanting to have a drink when I am with friends who drink
Emotional	Wanting to smoke marijuana to feel less anxious

Keep this list handy and add to it as you become more aware of your cravings. Refer to this list when you start working out strategies to help you manage these different types of cravings.

Four Reasons Addictions Are Hard to Break

Just because cravings are very common doesn't make them any easier to manage. If they were, we wouldn't be writing this book or devoting our lives to helping people overcome them—and you would not feel you need to read such a book.

It helps to understand what keeps people from trying to stop engaging in addictive behaviors in the first place.

First, you may be afraid that you will fail at managing cravings. Many who have a hard time managing cravings believe it reflects something negative about us. Virtually everyone experiences hard-to-control cravings—it's part of being human! Managing them is a process you can learn, though it may take many tries to master it. Remember this as you embark on your new journey.

Second, you may be afraid that you can't handle your cravings—a common barrier to recovery from substance dependency. You may be concerned that if you give up the substance, you won't know how to handle the craving—with potentially terrible consequences. You may have thoughts like *I may go crazy if I can't drink*, or *If I don't give in to a craving I won't be able to handle my anxiety*. Such thoughts are normal, and thankfully you too can learn to manage cravings successfully without any negative consequences. You do not need to drink to manage your anxiety, and you will not go crazy if you resist a craving. Cravings are normal, and they don't have to dictate your life.

Third, many of us don't know how to give up an addiction. That's also okay and normal. You likely didn't become addicted overnight—it happened over time. How interesting that it can take a long time to develop an addiction yet we may expect to overcome it immediately. Getting over an addiction and managing cravings does not have to take as long as it took us to get to where we are now, yet it needs *some* time and effort. You will learn the steps to quit engaging in an addiction and better managing your cravings.

Finally, many of us have a hard time viewing ourselves as someone who doesn't engage in an addiction. We see ourselves as a chocolate addict, a smoker, an alcoholic, or a drug user. We have engaged in addictions for many years; it has become a way of defining ourselves. It can be hard to see past that. We will touch on this important topic later in the book, helping you to see yourself in a different light—not as someone defined by your addiction.

EXERCISE: Our Myths About Cravings

Our minds can convince us of many possible bad things if we let go of addictions or if cravings show up. Consider what your mind tells you. Write some of these thoughts in a notebook or on the sheet provided with the online free tools (http://www.newharbinger.com/48336).

Are these just common myths that your mind has accepted?

Now let's review some common myths and see if any match up with yours.

Five Myths About Managing Cravings

Specific myths about managing cravings may be keeping you from understanding more about how to move past them. Have you believed any of these, or feel they've influenced how you have managed cravings?

Myth #1: Giving in to the Cravings Decreases Stress

You may think giving in makes you feel good, because of the instant relief you feel. But giving in never solves the source of your stress, and it may actually compound it. After the momentary relief, many people then feel bad about themselves, because their actions do not align with what is really important to them. Research shows that people who engage in addictive behaviors experience more stress than those who do not, and those who quit addictive behaviors experience less stress than those who don't. There are healthier ways to manage stress, and we will discuss alternative, more beneficial strategies.

Myth #2: Managing Cravings Is All About Willpower

Many think that if we just try harder to manage our cravings, we will finally overcome them. Often we blame ourselves for not having enough willpower, feeling destined to keep making the same bad decisions. There is nothing wrong with struggling to manage cravings. Managing cravings is not about willpower or any other aspect of our character.

Let's instead consider how you have been managing cravings. If you keep struggling with them, you'll keep feeling at war with them. Perhaps there are different, more effective strategies to try. We offer a different approach that has helped many people feel more capable of experiencing cravings, even embracing them, and making decisions based on what is important to them, rather than on the pull of the craving.

Myth #3: Having Cravings Means We Need What We Crave

Fact: your body does not need drugs and alcohol. But the addiction to these substances programs your brain to keep saying *You need it.* And that if you don't get what you *need,* terrible things will happen to you. None of that is true, but the addiction can be very convincing. For food, which *is* a necessity of life, it's a bit different; if you have a particular nutritional deficiency, your body will seek those nutrients. But cravings for salty, sugary, and fatty foods generally don't fall in this category. As with drugs and alcohol, consuming these foods stimulates the brain's pleasure receptors. But that doesn't mean that your body needs these unhealthy foods to survive and thrive—or even to feel pleasure.

Myth #4: We Should Be Able to Control Our Cravings

We have been taught that we should be able to control our thoughts, including cravings. This is easier said than done. When you try to control specific thoughts, often you end up thinking about them more. What if we told you to not think about a beautiful sunset? Don't think about the gorgeous flaming colors you would see with the sun going down. Go ahead— try your best to not think about it. Push it away. How is that working for you? If you're like most people, that thought is not so easy to get rid of once you tell yourself you can't have it. Now think about not eating chocolate, not smoking, not gambling. *Don't have that craving.* Chances are that craving will only be more intense. That's the problem with trying to control cravings.

Myth #5: We Need to Stop Having Cravings in Order to Move Forward and Change Our Lives

Again, cravings are a normal part of everyday life, just like other thoughts and feelings. It is impossible to rid our lives of all cravings. We *can* reduce their frequency, which we will work with you to do, but our aim is not to eliminate them. That is impossible. Imagine if we had no cravings at all? How would that help or harm us? Imagine we had no cravings for food. We might forget to eat, with serious consequences. We don't want cravings to be overwhelming, but we also don't want to get rid of cravings altogether.

But having cravings does not mean that you have to act on them. Your life does not have to be run by cravings. We will help you recognize that you have a choice. You can still move forward and change your life for the better in the presence of cravings. Once we accept the presence of cravings in our lives, we can turn our attention toward what is important to us. We start to recognize the choices we have and can take actions to have better lives, relationships, and well-being. This is the approach, based on the ACT principles, that we will ask you to take.

We Can Choose How to Manage Cravings

Now that you better understand why cravings occur, why you've had trouble managing cravings, and some common myths about managing cravings, let's discuss how to move forward. Learning how to manage cravings is a key part of your plan to overcoming addictions. Although you don't have a choice as to *whether* you will experience cravings, you can choose what to do when they show up. The moment between craving and action is where you can make that important choice.

Through the new approach you'll learn in this book, you will

- Learn to not act on unpleasant thoughts, feelings, sensations— and the cravings they trigger—but to experience them for what they are: as thoughts, feelings, sensations, and cravings.

- Become able to stop struggling with cravings, as you learn that they need not drive what you do.

- Expand your capacity to accomplish important goals that your craving-driven habits may have been keeping you from.

Ground Rules for Success

Before we begin teaching you these craving management methods, let's talk about some ground rules for success.

Rule one: *Be gentle with yourself* on this learning journey. It will likely take many trials to find what works for you and what doesn't. Every attempt you make, even if not successful, is an important learning experience. None are "failed" attempts. Although some people are successful on their first attempt, for most of us it takes many before we learn to successfully manage our cravings. We can get stuck on language like "I failed" and not see the value of every attempt. As you learn your triggers for cravings, you will come to know which management strategies work for you and which are less helpful. If you learn that something doesn't work for you, you can try something new.

Rule two: *It is okay to have mixed feelings about managing cravings.* Feeling ambivalent about giving up an addiction is normal. Certain foods, alcohol, drugs, or tobacco may have given you comfort for a long time, even if they have been destructive in your life. It is normal to both want to stop engaging in addictions and also be anxious or sad about the changes required. Ambivalence does not mean you can't do it. But it's important to be honest with yourself about how you feel.

Rule three: *The decision to learn how to manage cravings better and give up an addiction is yours to make.* No one can force you to quit eating what isn't good for you, drinking, using tobacco; you have to want to do it. Your motivation will inevitably go up and down—from day to day, even hour to hour, maybe even moment to moment! We will point you to strategies to help keep your motivation and commitment up and keep what is important close to your heart. However, this is ultimately up to you and your timeline. We look forward to helping you make the changes that you want to make in your life.

CHAPTER 2

Why Should We Give Up or Continue Addictions?

Kap   *I picked up smoking when I was in college. My buddy handed me one on a break, and I gave it a try. It seemed like everyone else was doing it, so why not? Back then, I didn't have strong cravings. I could take it or leave it. But over time, the cravings for cigarettes kept getting stronger and stronger. I was using it to control how I felt in my life. If I was sad or angry, I'd reach for a cigarette to distract myself and "calm down." On the hard days it became my friend. It is always there, and it made me feel good. It helped me relax, get my mind off of things. But I knew it wasn't good for me. Every time I tried to quit, I just gave in to the cravings. It was like they were in control of me.*

A good place to start when trying to manage cravings is to understand how they developed in the first place and why they still occur. Here we meet Kap, who has been struggling to quit smoking. His story may ring a bell, as you may have had similar experiences regardless of the substance you crave. To better manage cravings, we'll first review many reasons that people still engage in addictive behaviors and then review reasons to change how we approach these behaviors.

A Tiger We Continue to Feed

For many people, engaging in substance use didn't start as full-blown addiction. We usually pick it up casually, as Kap presents above. You may be mindlessly eating unhealthy food and then start to eat it more often. A friend might have passed you your first cigarette and you took your first puff, putting it down without any intention of using it again. But you do it again, and again, and then you are smoking regularly. You may have been at a party and had your first drink or joint, but then you use in more social situations and finally find yourself using it privately, in your own home, more often than you would like. It seems harmless enough in the beginning; we can take it or leave it. Over time, the addiction starts to take hold, and cravings become more intense.

We can think of cravings in the beginning as a baby tiger cub (Hayes, 2005). You get this baby tiger and take care of it—it's cute and harmless. The cub is not threatening at all. After all, it's just a baby. Over time, you start to become a little more concerned about the tiger as it grows bigger—it could bite and hurt you. To make sure that you keep the tiger satisfied, you go to the fridge and feed it some meat. Sure enough, if you throw it some meat it becomes preoccupied with its meal and leaves you alone. But the tiger continues to grow. Next time, it's hungrier and scarier. What do you do? You throw it some meat again. Now you feed it not because it is cute and you feel sorry for it, but because you feel your life may be at stake if you do not. You do this over and over to make the tiger leave you alone. But the more you feed the tiger, the bigger it gets, and the more frightened you feel. You hope that one day it'll leave you alone. But it doesn't leave—it just gets bigger, hungrier, and more frightening. One day, you walk to your fridge and you don't have any more meat left to give—at this point, there's nothing left to feed it but yourself!

This is how cravings become more and more intense over time. If we continue to feed the tiger, the tiger keeps coming back for more. The only way to get the tiger to leave is to stop feeding it!

Reasons to Use Substances

But there are other reasons that addictions take hold and cravings take control over our lives.

Reason to Use #1: Social Situations

We often use substances and experience cravings in social situations. Many people start and even continue to use substances like tobacco, alcohol, and drugs because of peer pressure. Kap tells us that a friend of his just passed him a cigarette during a break when in college. It seemed that all his friends were doing it, and initially he may have smoked to fit in. Our addictions may start because peers are doing it and then are maintained because the people we spend time with continue to use these substances. We may believe that if we stop we wouldn't fit in with them anymore. And it can be tough to stop using when our use and cravings happen in the company of others. But stopping is definitely possible—and you can do it too.

Reason to Use #2: Feeling Good

Substances like high-calorie foods, tobacco, alcohol, and drugs make us feel good. As mentioned in the last chapter, they release a powerful neurotransmitter, dopamine, that produces feelings of pleasure. Drinking alcohol can give us a buzz that we like, drugs and tobacco can give us a high, and chocolate's taste is pleasurable. How intense the "high" is depends on the substance; some mind-altering drugs produce pretty powerful pleasurable feelings that can be difficult to resist. We may start to use such substances because they make us feel good. After some time, we need more and more of the substance to get the same feeling that we had when we first started using it. This effect is called *tolerance*. For example, that first cigarette of the day can produce a little high that we never quite achieve with later smokes. However, we keep giving in to cravings so that we don't have to feel the craving anymore—eventually, we just keep using to feel as normal as possible. When we don't use the substances, we don't feel good at all (usually because of withdrawal symptoms).

Reason to Use #3: Managing Our Emotions

As detailed in the last chapter, many of us use food, tobacco, alcohol, and drugs to help us cope with our emotions, like anxiety, stress, depression, and anger. Remember Amy, who consumed food and especially sweets when under stress? We reach for these substances to distract us from strong emotions. We often feel like we need a break, and these substances will briefly take our mind off our troubles. The main issue with this approach is that it never actually solves the source of our stress, and in time, cravings become an additional source of stress. This stress increases with addiction and additional feelings of guilt, sadness, disappointment, betrayal, and so on. And by not actually facing the source of our troubling emotions, we are not dealing with it effectively, which prolongs and even increases our feelings of distress.

Reason to Use #4: Managing Pain

Similar to emotional pain, we often use substances like food, tobacco, alcohol, and drugs to manage our physical pain. We are seeking a way to distract or numb ourselves. It does work in the short term, which is why many of us find it hard to stop using substances to alleviate pain. In the long term it makes the problem worse. Eating unhealthy food only makes us gain more weight, which compounds our pain. Smoking interferes with the absorption of pain medication and impairs our circulation, preventing effective healing. Alcohol and drug use lead to significant health problems that exacerbate physical pain. But it's hard for us to look past the short-term relief of using substances to see the long-term consequences.

Reason to Use #5: Poor Self-Esteem

When we don't feel good about ourselves, we are more likely to do harmful things, like overeat, smoke, drink, and use drugs. Sometimes we don't think we deserve better. We keep internalizing negative messages— *I'm not good enough.* These thoughts keep us hooked into harmful practices because we think we aren't worthy of a good life. So we have a drink and briefly feel more confident, able to talk to someone interesting at a bar. Yet this habit does not increase our self-esteem, and we now believe the only way to talk to others is by first having a drink. Our self-esteem actually worsens, particularly when compounded by the problems stemming from substance use and addiction.

Reason to Use #6: To Be More Productive

We might turn to stimulants to get more energy, smoke or drink because we believe it improves our attention, or use alcohol to feel more relaxed in challenging social situations. But over time these behaviors actually make us less productive. As with our other reasons for using substances, there is a downside: eventually we must use just to maintain a baseline of feeling "normal." Using stimulants can take control of our lives, and work becomes less important. Alcohol starts to interfere with work performance—we need it in the morning just to avoid feeling bad. We may not show up to work or school, with serious consequences.

Reasons to Change

Now let's think about the flip side—why would we want to give up our substance use? You may already have given this some thought. Here are some common reasons why people decide to make a change in their lives, to manage their cravings or stop an addictive behavior.

Reason to Change #1: Becoming Healthier

Addictions have a tremendously bad impact on our health. Poor eating habits, tobacco use, and substance use are among the most health-damaging behaviors we can engage in. Obesity caused by excessive and/or unhealthy eating is linked to high blood pressure, diabetes, heart disease, stroke, and many types of cancers. Similarly, tobacco use is associated with deaths from heart disease, stroke, cancer, and chronic obstructive pulmonary disease. Heavy long-term use of alcohol can lead to liver damage. Heavy alcohol use is associated with an irregular heartbeat, high blood pressure, stroke, cancer, and neurological problems. Drug misuse can also cause a number of serious health issues, including kidney damage, liver damage, abnormal heart rate, heart attacks, stroke, and neurological problems. But when we take steps to manage cravings and addictions more effectively, we can substantially improve our health.

Reason to Change #2: Living Longer

Unsurprisingly, given the negative impact of substance use on our bodies, if we engage in addictive behaviors, particularly long and heavy use, we risk early death. Heavy alcohol use is the cause of 10 percent of deaths among working-age adults in the United States—ninety-three thousand Americans each year (Centers for Disease Control, 2020)—and the loss of up to nineteen years of potential life per individual (Chikritzhs et al., 2001). One study of heroin addicts found their lives were shortened by an average of eighteen years (Smyth, Hoffman, Fan, & Hser, 2007). Severely obese adults aged twenty to thirty-nine can expect to lose about eight years of potential life span to obesity (Lung, Jan, Tan, Killedar, & Hayes, 2019). But by limiting overeating, improving our diet, limiting or stopping drinking, and eliminating the use of substances like tobacco and drugs, we can regain a substantial amount of that potential time. Compared to lifelong nonsmokers, smokers lose about ten years of life. Quit smoking and you regain that potential. For instance, compared to people who continue to smoke, if you quit smoking between ages twenty-five and thirty-four, you'll gain ten more years; between thirty-five and forty-four, nine more years; and between forty-five and fifty-four, about six more years (Jha et al., 2013).

Reason to Change #3: Feeling Healthier

Due to the physical toll that addictions take on our bodies, we often don't feel as good as we could. When we stop giving in to cravings and letting addictions have control in our lives, our bodies have a chance to become healthier, and then we feel healthier. Many people report having more energy, breathing better, coughing less. Giving up addictions can help you feel healthier for the rest of your life. In addition to gaining years of life, it is important to consider that when we make changes and quit substance use, we gain improved quality of life and well-being. Thus, we not only extend years of our lives but we ensure that we have healthier lives and less disability during our remaining years.

Reason to Change #4: Managing Pain

Freeing yourself from addictions is one of the best things you can do to better manage your pain—even if you took up the substance for pain relief. Managing your cravings better and giving up addictions will likely help you manage your pain. Giving up overeating or unhealthy food can help you lose weight, reducing pressure on your joints, the hips, knees, spine, and supporting muscle groups, which can help ease arthritis pain, for example. When you stop smoking, circulation improves, which helps your body heal better. Finally, when you quit substance use, you may experience better results from prescribed pain medications, as they are better absorbed, potentially enabling a lower dose and fewer side effects.

Reason to Change #5: Improving Mental Health

Although we may think substances help us manage our mental health, they actually make it worse. Giving up addictions is strongly linked to better mental health. For instance, people who eat healthier are less likely to be depressed or anxious. People who do not smoke or have quit have less stress in their lives than people who smoke. People who give up problematic drinking and drug use experience a substantial improvement in their well-being and quality of life.

Reason to Change #6: More Money

Addictive behaviors can be expensive! We may spend a lot of money on fast food or ordering out. Cigarettes only get more expensive, consuming more of a smoker's income. Similarly, drugs and alcohol can be expensive. Without the drain of these expenses, you'll have more money in your pocket. Imagine what you could put that money into. With the savings over time, you could go on a relaxing vacation, buy a new car, even find a better place to live. We know real-life examples. Maria had a client who quit smoking, and with the money she saved in one year she started college. Megan had clients who were able to buy their own home with the money they used to spend on cigarettes.

Reason to Change #7: Relationships

Relationships often improve as a result of giving up addictive behaviors. If our health is negatively affected by substance use and unhealthy eating, we can't be there for the people we care about. We may need to have others care for us, which can take a toll on those relationships. Using substances also is a frequent cause of arguments in families and between friends. Friends and family often worry about our poor diet, smoking, drinking, and drug use. When we manage our cravings better and free ourselves from addictive behaviors, we make our family and friends proud. We stop feeling like social outcasts; our interactions with our loved ones improve, and we can restore healthy relationships.

Reason to Change #8: Freedom

Managing cravings better also leads to more freedom in our lives. Our cravings no longer control us. We don't have to worry about whether we have cigarettes or where we will be able to smoke next. We're no longer concerned about running out of alcohol or drugs, or where we can get the next fix. We don't have to listen to cravings telling us what to do and how to do it. We have more time to do what we want to do and the freedom to be who we want to be. Clients tell us that while using substances they would say and do things that did not represent who they are: lying about using, hiding their addiction from friends or family, owing money to others, missing appointments and responsibilities. Changing addictive behaviors gives us the freedom to be who we truly want to be without the substances clouding our judgments or choices.

Reason to Change #9: Being Proud of Yourself

Regaining personal pride and self-esteem is a key reason that many people give up addictions and manage their cravings better. It feels good to know that you are doing something to improve your health and quality of life. Megan worked with an individual who initially quit smoking because he needed money. When asked if he would go back to smoking once he got more money, he said that no doubt he would. Three weeks after quitting, he received a large check, which made him more financially secure. She asked him, "Now that you have more money, are you going back to smoking?" He said, "No! I am too proud of my accomplishment!" His reasons for quitting smoking had changed; now his pride was his most important reason for managing his cravings and being free from smoking. Being proud of yourself is one of the best ways to improve self-esteem and self-image. Clients often tell us that once they achieved an addiction-free life, they become more social, fun, life-loving individuals.

EXERCISE: Reviewing Your Reasons

Let's review your reasons for using substances compared to reasons not to use substances. In a separate notebook or using the worksheet with the online free tools, compare your reasons for either. After you list them, rate their weight (that is, their importance) for you, from 0 (not at all important) to 10 (extremely important).

Now sum up the weight for each of the columns: one score for reasons for using substances and one for reasons to stop using.

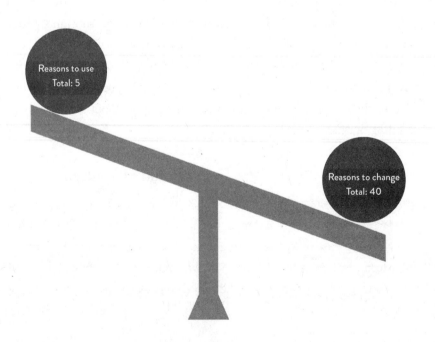

What do you think of your list? Are your reasons for giving up substances weightier than your reasons for continuing their use, or the opposite? This can give you a good picture of how motivated you are to better manage your cravings and addictive behaviors. The preceding figure represents Kap's sums and conclusions. Now you've got a good starting point for understanding where you are in your journey to better manage your cravings. You can start to think about how to make your reasons for giving up substances more important than your reasons to continue. Can you accept your reasons for using but still move in the direction of what is important to you? Remember, this effort is completely up to you! These are *your* reasons for changing your life. No one can choose these reasons for you. We hope this is a good beginning for you.

Bringing It All Together

- We do not have to keep feeding our addictive behaviors by giving in to cravings. We can make a different choice.

- There are many reasons to use and many reasons to change. We each balance our reasons—but when this balance tips toward what we care about, this is when we can make positive changes in our life.

Bringing Our Learning to Life

As we proceed with the next few chapters, continue referring to your reasons to use and reasons to change. Notice if and how their weight changes as you start to use new skills to help you manage cravings.

In the next chapter, we'll discuss what's really important to you in your life and tie it back to your reasons for managing cravings and addictions better. Even if your motivation is low at the moment, we hope to help you to increase your motivation to make needed changes in your life.

CHAPTER 3

Why Manage Craving and Change Addictive Behaviors?

Changing Even If You Do Not Want To

Amy *Food gives me comfort. It makes me feel good when I am stressed, when I am tired, when I've had a terrible day. The sweet taste of ice cream or chocolate makes me feel good inside, and for a few moments all the craziness in my life disappears. When the craving for sweets shows up, it makes me feel so good to reach out and eat that craved food. Just for a few moments I feel happy… I do not want to lose these moments of happiness!*

Kap *For a long time, cigarettes have been my friends. They were always with me, silently there when I needed them, not judging me or saying anything bad about me. I could count on them to make me feel better.*

Most things we do in life have a purpose. We brush our teeth in the morning because we care for our dental health and want to prevent cavities. We may go to work every day because we like our job, or we care about the work we do, or we need that weekly or monthly paycheck. We may call our parents because we care about them. Consuming substances—food, alcohol, drugs, or cigarettes—is no different; each serves a function. And we may give in to cravings and smoke, use drugs, drink alcohol, consume craved food for reasons we explored in the last chapter.

As we learn why we give in to cravings—the "whys" behind our substance use—we can discover ways to better manage and overcome our cravings and begin to live the sort of life we want to be living. This will help us figure out our values, which, in turn, give us the whys for changing and can act as our compass to find our way when cravings show up.

Finding the Why for Making a Change

We have worked with many individuals just like Amy and Kap. Like them, most express that they use their particular addictive substance because it offers them something, usually some form of relief or pleasure. If using substances provides pleasure—and for some people, dealing with difficult life situations, this seems to be their only source of pleasure—why should they give up that pleasure?

This quandary pulls people back into addictive behaviors again and again. If these behaviors were not pleasurable, it would be easy to not do them. If we did not enjoy eating chocolates, we would not eat them. If smokers or individuals who use drugs did not find pleasure in smoking or using, they would not smoke or use. If people didn't get pleasure from eating unhealthy food, they wouldn't do it. These behaviors tend to be reinforced by the pleasure we experience immediately after we engage in them, even if the pleasure is only short lived and even if soon we may feel guilty, angry, or sad that we indulged in that craving and ate the cake, smoked another cigarette, or had that drink. This immediate pleasure or relief from stress and other unwanted emotions is enough to maintain the behavior. The next time we are in a similar stressful situation, we experience that craving and are more likely to indulge in it. The next time we want to take a break from stress, a craving is likely to show up. If Kap picks up another cigarette, it will give him immediate relief and pleasure. This forms a vicious cycle: the person believes that they *need* that substance for the pleasure it will provide; they use the substance, which immediately provides pleasure; and they become seduced into believing that this is the only way to feel pleasure, so they keep going back to the substance.

This chapter is about helping you explore your whys. Why give up something that provides pleasure or has a function for you? Why make the necessary changes in your life to become addiction-free? Why attempt something that may be difficult? Finding these whys can help motivate you to make a change, and motivate you again when making that change gets hard.

To start exploring these whys, let's try a little exercise we call The Game of Life (adapted from Hayes & Ciarrochi, 2015; Nikolaou & Karekla, 2017).

EXERCISE: The Game of Life

Choose five numbers from 1 through 80 and write them down in a notebook.

Now turn to The Game of Life table in the online free tools (http://www .newharbinger.com/48336). Find your chosen numbers, and in your notebook enter the words that your numbers correspond with.

How did you do? Did you find success, or were you heading for destruction? Did you find love or loneliness? Loyalty or betrayal? Addiction or freedom?

How would you feel if what you randomly picked was how your life would be?

Did you like having a random exercise dictate how your life would be, or would you prefer to be the one making the choices for your life?

If you want to be the one choosing, go through the table again, but this time choose how you would want your life to be. You can pick any of the squares with things you'd like in your life.

What did you pick? Write in your notebook the words you picked from the table.

Here is what Amy got when we played the game: Rejected, Create, In debt, Love, Betrayal. She liked Create and Love. The rest disturbed her. She did not want to be rejected or to reject others, fall into debt, or betray and be betrayed by others. She felt relief when we asked her to choose for herself what mattered to her. She had a hard time choosing just five, but these were her top choices: Love, Caring, Travel, Respected, and Security.

Kap got the following the first time around: Be poor, Unemployed, Brave, Liar, and Fame. He said none of these really represented him or what he would want his life to be about. Instead, he chose Caring, Create, Loyalty, Hardworking, and Influence.

A Values-Based Life

We all have dreams of how we'd like our life to unfold. When other people try to tell us what those dreams should look like, it rarely matches with what we really want or who we are. We want to be free: in control of who we are and how we live our life.

Our choices in The Game of Life are related to our *values*.

Values are our heart's deepest desires. They are those qualities we cherish in ourselves, others, and our relationships. Values are the core elements of our life, the things that give our lives meaning and purpose. They are those characteristics that motivate us to do things even when these things are hard or we do not feel like doing them at the time.

Values aren't the same as goals—and that's an important point for our work together. Goals are usually temporary events with an end point (one of our goals might be to become a full professor). You can put a goal on a to-do list, achieve it or not, and then tick it off the list. Values can't just be ticked off a list.

Let us demonstrate values with an example from Amy's story. Amy said one of her most important values is being an engaged, present, giving, active, and supportive mother. This doesn't mean she will do one supportive thing for her kids and then tick "be a supportive mother" off of her to-do list forever. Nailed it; never have to do that again. Definitely not! Being this kind of mother requires continuous effort.

So on days when Amy is too stressed and too tired to move, on days when she has worked late, with back-to-back meetings and colleagues constantly asking for help, when she gets home all she wants to do is just sit on the couch, eat a craved food, and not move or talk for at least fifteen minutes. If you have kids, you will immediately guess that this dream never materializes. As soon as she gets home, her kids run up to tell her about their day, to present all sorts of problems they had to face at school with their friends or teachers, to tell her about the party or activity they have to go to, to ask her to cook something specific for dinner or play a new game with them. All she wants is to "sink" into the couch and eat Twinkies! How is this consistent with her value of being an engaged, present, giving, supporting mother? It is not. Yet she has a *choice.*

Even if she is tired, if being an engaged, present, giving, active, supporting mother is important, what will she choose to do? In the process of connecting with her values, Amy started to explore her choices. She started to recognize that each moment is a *choice moment* (adapted from Harris, 2019; Karekla, 2010), and she can choose to go in the direction of her values or in a different direction, usually that of her addictive behaviors. Amy started to exercise her *choice moments* and started to choose to listen, to respond, to commit to being a taxi driver, to cook, to play. However difficult the task feels at the time, she does it because it is in accordance with what she values. So she chooses "valuing" over the couch and the Twinkies.

We particularly care about the *verb* "valuing" and not so much the noun "value." We make this distinction here because we want to emphasize *action* and our ability to choose our actions.

Values also help keep us going when things get hard, and especially when those cravings show up. Values make doing the difficult thing worth all the effort. Goals can be useful when we travel along our values-based life path. They can help us head in the directions we want to go. When we live a values-based life, we can achieve a goal, and there will be another one to follow. Amy can choose to play a game with her kids (goal), which can be achieved and finished. She then may choose to engage in another valued activity (such as helping her children with a problem they are facing); doing this is another goal in the service of being an engaged, present, giving, supporting mother (value). The danger is that once we achieve a goal, sometimes we halt further progress toward our valued path. For example, a person's choosing not to drink alcohol during a meal with the family does not mean they've exercised their choice for the day, lived up to their values, and need not do anything else. To live a values-based life, we need to remain consistently engaged with our values and choose ongoing valued goals and actions.

Values Exploration

Each of us has not just one, but many values. This is why we asked you to choose a number of words from The Game of Life table. Before we proceed, let's try to find these valued areas for you. The first indication of important things for you may arise from your responses to that game. Let's explore this a bit more.

Maria recalls: When my son was in kindergarten, on Mother's Day we mothers got invited to go to the school, where the children had prepared a celebration for us. My son was so excited for me to attend so he could show me all that he had prepared! The celebration started with the children singing a song about the mother being the most important person in any child's life, always the one who is there and cares for them, and so on. The children were adorable, singing and smiling to their mothers as they sang their song. Next, they each stood in front of the class to recite a few sentences about their mother. The first kid said, "I love my mother, and I wish she would go cycling with me." The next: "My mother is great, except when she is yelling at me to clean up and eat. I wish she would speak to me nicely just like she asks me to speak to her." The next kid: "My mother has a very important job, which gives us money to buy things. I wish that she would sometimes have time to play with me with the gifts she buys me." This went on and on. I was mortified! Why? It hit home that though these kids offered gratitude to their mothers, they also expressed what really matters to them in their relationships with their mothers. This made me wonder: *What type of a mother do I want to be? What sort of relationship do I want to have with my children? What would I want my son to say about me?* So we ask you now to imagine such a celebration for you on Mother's or Father's Day or Husband's or Wife's Day, Friend's Day, and so on. What would you want the people in your life to say about you?

EXERCISE: What Is Important to You?

Take a few minutes to think about—what is important to you. What kinds of things do you want to live for? What interests you? Answer each of these questions in your notebook.

What are your deepest wants and desires? What kind of person do you want to be? What kind of relationships do you want to have? If you could be free to do whatever you want, what would you do? These aren't easy questions to answer, but they're very important. Take some time to ponder them and write your responses in your notebook.

Within these sentences you will start to find clues about your values and what is important for you. Don't worry if you don't have all the answers. No need to justify your choices; they are yours and yours alone. The Game of Life we played earlier will help us work together to explore your values. Then we can make them more specific to help you choose what to do now and in the future.

To complete the Values Exercise, please download the table available in the online free tools (http://www.newharbinger.com/48336). In it we list various values that different individuals have told us are important to them. Just as each of us has personal preferences for food, music, art, hobbies, and so on, we each can also have different values, and some values may be less or more important to each of us.

The Values Exercise table has three columns; complete each column in its entirety before proceeding to the next column. For each of the values listed, rate on a scale from 0, "not important at all," to 10, "very important." Feel free to add any other values that are important to you.

As you go through the table, notice that your mind may react to your ratings or tell you to modify them because you may not have been living in accordance to these values. For example, love may be an important value for you, but if you have not been very loving lately, your mind may tell you to not rank this value as important. Tell your mind that in the next column you will be able to make a judgment, but for the first column we want you to dig deep and be truthful.

Once you complete the first column, go on to the second. Think back over the past two weeks and consider how much reward or meaning you have gotten from this value in that time.

For the third column, go back through the list and consider how dealing with your cravings fits with each of the values.

How did it go? Did you find any difficulties in completing it? If yes, what were these difficulties about? What did you notice about your values and what is important to you? What sort of person do you want to be? How does giving in to craving fit with these values?

Our clients often notice a few things: their rankings in columns 1 and 2 do not match, and dealing with cravings becomes very important for living in accordance with their values. For example, Kap highly rated the value of honesty, but the test revealed that he continuously felt that he was cheating himself and his family when he gave in to cravings and smoked. Dealing with the craving and not smoking was thus immensely important to him in the service of living a life of honesty.

Recognizing the differences in your ratings between the columns is the first step to starting to deal with cravings and change your behavior.

Values and Competing Choices

As you explore your values, you will notice that some of them may compete with each other or clash, which can confuse us as to how to behave or what to choose. Let's return to Amy's after-work choice: sinking into the couch and eating Twinkies, or engaging with her kids. If Amy wants to be an engaged, caring mother and live in accordance with her values, she should pick the latter choice. However, it is not so easy. Should Amy *always* choose to serve her kids over her own need for rest and relaxation? Of course not. Being healthy is another important value for Amy, and it involves taking a break and decompressing (as well as exercising, eating healthy, preventive care, and so on, as shown in the following figure).

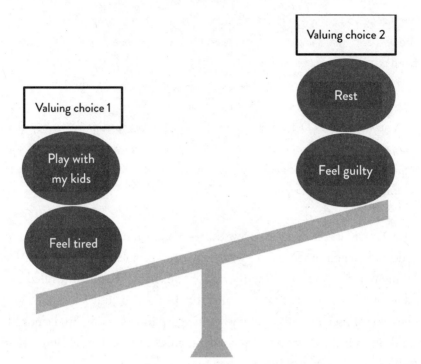

These times of tough choices between values are called *values conflicts.* On the one hand, it is great to have such choices; they mean you have valued areas in your life. On the other hand, having valuing choices (that is, choices about how to act in line with our values) pulls us in different directions; no matter which direction we choose, we may not feel completely content, or we may experience troublesome feelings of guilt or tiredness. If Amy were to choose playing with her kids over relaxing, she might feel even more tired or start to get irritated. If she were to choose relaxing over playing, she might feel guilty. It may feel like a no-win situation. It may feel like we are on a seesaw—something we loved doing as a kid that nowadays makes us all too dizzy.

What to do? Which side of the seesaw will prevail? Research demonstrates that problems arise when we deviate from our valued path or when we choose one valued area over others more frequently or for longer periods of time. If Amy were to continuously choose playing with her kids over resting, she would end up burning out. If she were to always choose resting over playing with her kids, she would miss out on some of the most important moments with them. So when we have a values conflict, the trick is to be flexible and not always rigidly choose the same value over the other. Of course with substances (not food), we hope that over time, using the skills you will learn in this book, when cravings show up you'll choose to not indulge but instead make other values-based choices.

EXERCISE: Valuing Choices Seesaw

Take a few moments now to consider the different valuing choices you usually face and may struggle with. We would suggest you complete the Valuing Choices Seesaw (a free online tool) and start to both explore your valuing choices and also recognize choices you already make. If you learn that you tend to choose one value over others, recognize that as what we call a *choice moment* and then choose what your next values-based moves will be.

Of course, you can prioritize your values and choose to focus on one at a time. This does not mean the other values aren't still important; it just means that at *this* moment you choose to focus on this one; in another choice moment you can choose to prioritize another value.

Feelings, Choices, and Cravings

It's also important to address our feelings—especially feelings that we consider negative or bothersome. These are the ones that as humans we naturally try to get away from: pain, stress, anxiety, sadness, anger, fatigue, guilt—the list goes on. However, the feelings we consider positive can also get in our way. If we try to cling too much to feeling happy, joyous, contented, or satisfied, we can fall into the trap of not being able to feel these all the time (nobody can!), and then we blame ourselves for not managing to feel them or believe that we cannot make choices in our lives until we feel these positive feelings (for example, I cannot play with my kids unless I feel rested and happy).

Our motivation to do something is often driven by these feelings (expecting to have the positive and not the negative ones in order to act).

These feelings (also called *emotional goals*) are not values. Making choices based on feelings may lead us astray and away from values-based living. Actually, this is what cravings do. We postpone living a values-based life until our cravings disappear or are "fixed." Craving is actually a feeling that usually shows up along with the thought *When this craving goes away, I will be able to quit smoking, taking drugs, bingeing, overeating...* The problem is, we have little control over our feelings. If we ask you now to stop loving your most loved person on earth, could you do it? If we ask you to feel an intense craving to eat manure, would you be able to bring on such a craving? (We will explore this topic more in the next chapter, Controlling Cravings Doesn't Work.)

What we can control, however, is valuing—the actions we choose to take based on our values. This is important because what we value is always there, within our hearts, to inspire us, to help and guide us in making choices and taking actions. So Amy may *feel* tired and still *choose* to play with her children. Kap may *feel* a craving for cigarettes and still *choose* to not smoke while talking with his friends.

Others, Choices, and Cravings

Values are about how *you* want and choose to behave. Notice the emphasis on *you*. Your values have nothing to do with those of others. For example, you may have picked love as an important value for you because you want to be loved. This is a natural desire. Yet whether others will extend their love to us is not within our control. All we can do is be loving ourselves, openly loving and caring with those we care about. As a result, others may return our love. But we cannot just sit around waiting, demanding that others be loving toward us. We can take actions to increase the likelihood of being loved, respected, cared for, but our actions won't guarantee that we will actually experience these. The question, then, is whether you are willing to *be loving* (an action on your part) because doing so is something you value, regardless of how others will behave in return. Will you be loving, caring, and honest because this is who you want to be?

Clients often tell us they are behaving based on their values and are choosing to not smoke, drink, overeat, or use, yet others may sabotage these efforts by bringing up cues that trigger cravings for the client. Digging deeper, we discover that the client has fallen into the trap of expecting others to behave in ways consistent with what *the client* values. Such expectations bring a stream of feelings, including cravings, that can sabotage your values-based living intention to better manage your addictive behaviors. Be aware of this issue and wary of expectations for others' behavior toward you. Our values are ours alone, and if they are important to us, we need to choose our behaviors for ourselves, not for what they can get us from others.

Choice Moment

Each moment offers a choice for how we will act, moving us either toward our values and what is important to us, or away from them. Each choice moment is critical, because how we choose to act will generate different outcomes. We call actions that move us toward our chosen values *toward actions*, whereas behaviors that serve to satisfy other motives (such as getting rid of cravings, fearful thoughts, or emotions), which tend to move us away from our values, we call *away actions*. We hope the skills you will learn in this book will help you increase your toward actions and decrease your away actions (see the figure). This figure is available as a handout in the online free tools (http://www.newharbinger.com/48336). You can add your values, identified earlier in this chapter, to the Values list box now. You'll be adding more to it in the coming chapters as you gain new knowledge and skills.

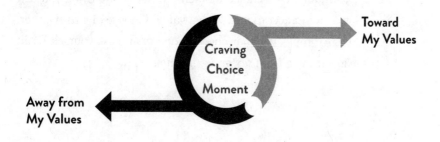

Bringing It All Together

Our values are important for these reasons:

- Values provide the why for choosing to do things that are difficult or hard—such as stopping behaviors we may not really want to change but know are harming us in some way (such as addictive behaviors). Values motivate us to keep going when cravings show up.

- Values are our internal compass, showing us the way when we get lost or feel stuck, when cravings pull us toward addiction.

- Values bring meaning and satisfaction to our lives when we live in accordance with them. We may not always be able to achieve our goals, overcome all obstacles, or eliminate cravings, but if we are on our valued-living path, then every step can be rewarding and satisfying.

- Living in accordance with our values helps us manage cravings and begin to change our behaviors, effectively and lastingly.

Bringing Our Learning to Life

It's time to put what you've learned and explored here into practice. As you go about your day, ask yourself: *Am I now acting on my values?*

- If yes, first congratulate yourself, then notice how it feels. What difference does it make in your life, your relationships, your cravings, and your addictive behaviors?

- If no, consider this a choice moment. What is one thing you can do now to act in accordance with a value? Choose one thing, then do it. For example, you may choose honesty and ask yourself *What is one honest thing I can say or do right now?*

Another suggestion: look at your list of values each morning and choose one—say, friendship—to prioritize that day. As you go about your day, search for opportunities to act based on this value. This can be infused into anything, even seemingly small things: a couple of friendly words, a smile, a phone call. Choose also to not give in to a craving by thinking about what is important for you (your values and the reasons you're trying to change) and following this valued-living path. Notice what effects valuing has on you and others.

In the next chapter, we will take a look at how controlling cravings often doesn't work. We'll discuss why this is usually problematic and introduce an alternative strategy: acceptance.

CHAPTER 4

Controlling Cravings Doesn't Work

Fai   *I am a chocolate lover. I know I have a sweet tooth. I have been the kind of lucky person who could always eat whatever they wanted without really gaining weight. Recently, however, I was diagnosed with diabetes, and for the first time I have to watch my diet and especially my sweets intake. For a few weeks I was doing really well; I was able to follow the healthy diet I was given. Then I lost my job. I was home all the time and coping with financial stress. Whenever I went into the kitchen or needed a break from the stress, I would immediately get a strong craving and rummage through my cupboards to find something sweet to eat. I found this very hard to control. The more I tried to put the cravings out of my mind, the more they took hold of me. I would think: I feel so stressed, I might as well feel happy while I eat whatever I want, and as soon as I ate the sweets, I would feel guilty and hate myself for what I'd done. Even though I tried my best to control my cravings, I was left feeling like I had no control over them at all.*

In the previous chapter we worked with values. How did that go for you? How is life when you live in accordance with your values? Did you notice a difference? We hope you also discovered what obstacles show up in your attempts to live according to what matters most to you. Cravings are common obstacles. In the next few chapters you'll learn various skills to help you manage your cravings and live a values-based life.

As you go through the book and start to practice new skills, you may experience some challenges. If you ever lose your way, remember your compass. Revisit your values to remind you why you are trying to deal with your cravings and change your behavior.

In this chapter, we'll learn how trying to control cravings can be a problem. The more Fai tried to push the cravings away, the more intense they became—a very common experience. Keeping this in mind, instead of controlling cravings, let's learn about new ways of managing them.

The Craving Control Paradox

Have you ever had a stone in your shoe, or felt a chill as the sun was setting and a light evening breeze started to blow, or taken a bite of food and realized it is rancid or spoiled? These are all situations that make us feel uncomfortable. How do we react? We want to relieve our discomfort: by removing the stone from our shoe, putting on a sweater, or spitting out the food. These good survival strategies give us a great evolutionary advantage and decrease the chances we'll get hurt. These avoidance strategies work well when it comes to events or situations happening in the world around us. What happens though when the things we want to avoid are inside of us? Like cravings?

EXERCISE: Ways We Try to Manage Cravings

Let's take some time to think about how we usually try to manage cravings. In a notebook, consider your past week and write down how many times you tried to manage cravings. Write specifically what you did to manage them. Make a note of whether these strategies worked for you or not.

If you are like many of us, you have undoubtedly tried many different strategies to get rid of your cravings:

• Pushing them out of your mind

• Thinking about something else

• Replacing thoughts of what you crave with other more appealing thoughts

Have the ways you've tried to manage your cravings worked? Maybe temporarily, but they do not really get rid of cravings; they only prolong them—it is like feeding the tiger again.

EXERCISE: Don't Think About...

When you try hard to push a thought away, it tends to stick around for much longer. Think about a big white elephant—huge body, big floppy ears, wrinkly white skin. Now stop thinking about it. No more thoughts of that white elephant! None at all for the next minute.

How'd you do? Did you banish that white elephant from your mind?

The elephant most likely persisted (or kept popping up) because the more we are told to consciously *not* think about something, the more our brain is compelled to think of it. When we *try* to suppress a thought or a feeling, it often comes back even stronger. The same thing happens when we try to push cravings away. If we tell ourself we can't have this thought, we have it. Same thing when we try to think a different thought. It may work momentarily, but we quickly realize we are thinking about the "white elephant" again. If we try to replace our craving thought with another, the craving thought is still there.

As we mentioned in chapter 1, we may have tried to rely on willpower to manage our cravings. If only we had more willpower, we could just walk away from them. And when we can't, we figure there is something wrong with us. But managing cravings is not about willpower. If we rely on willpower alone to manage cravings (some people describe "white-knuckling" it to get through), we might be successful for a little while, but we'll be left exhausted. And when you are exhausted that's often when you give in to those cravings and binge eat, chain smoke, and start using substances again. Willpower is not the answer.

It doesn't seem fair. The more we try to control our cravings, the harder it gets to do just that. It's like a rigged game that we can't win. That is how our inner world works. In the outside world we seem to have more control: we can avoid, change, or get rid of things we do not want or that bother us. But when it comes to our inner world, the rules seem reversed. Inside, the more we try to avoid or change things, the more potent and bothersome they become. We're left feeling depressed and guilty that we can't manage our cravings. But what you have been seeing as possible solutions to managing your cravings are actually part of the problem. Perhaps your dedicated efforts to control or get rid of cravings is only making the situation worse!

Now for another little exercise.

EXERCISE: Tactics Used to Control Cravings

In a quiet setting where you have time to yourself, think about all the tactics you use to control your craving thoughts and feelings. As each comes to mind, write it down in your notebook. Be honest—include everything you do, even if it's embarrassing. This is just for you. As you record, notice any emerging patterns— especially those of struggle and avoidance.

Now consider how much each of these tactics has actually helped you manage your cravings. Have any helped you achieve your goal: getting rid of cravings for good? Note whether any tactics worked for you in the short run (right at that moment) or in the long run.

Fai, for example, wrote these tactics: eating sweets, eating fast food, trying to not think about it, trying to distract myself, telling myself things like *You know better*. In the moment, she felt a little better—less stressed. In the long run, however, these completely failed and left her feeling more stressed, less able to control her cravings and herself, guilty, and even disgusted at herself. She realized her strategies did not work in the long run.

Because you are reading this book, we can confidently assume that your tactics have mostly failed. That is not your fault! You've done what you could, based on what you knew to do. Avoidance tactics seem to have some effect in the short run. When Fai gets a craving, she may avoid going into the kitchen so as not to dive into the fridge or grab chocolate from the cupboard. This may work for a little while, which enhances her belief that she can control the craving. However, the craving soon returns with more strength, along with rationalizing thoughts like *A little chocolate will not kill me*. What does Fai do then? She ends up consuming the craved food, then starts blaming herself for being weak and unable to overcome the cravings. This is the craving control paradox!

Consider this: what you've been seeing as possible solutions to managing cravings *may themselves be part of the problem.*

We are *not* saying you are to blame for this. Far from it! We are saying that maybe what you have learned to do to manage cravings is not what works. Does this mean there is nothing you can do? That you will always feel powerless over cravings? Of course not. There *are* things you can do— just not the same ones you have been trying.

The Rip Current of Cravings

Have you ever heard of rip currents? A rip current is somewhat like a tornado that happens under water. A rip current moves away from a beach, cutting through the incoming breaking waves. They can be quite dangerous for swimmers (and even those just wading); indeed, every year dozens of people drown when caught by a rip current, and thousands more must be rescued.

The craving control paradox we just discussed is like a rip current. When we are caught in it, it feels like we are drowning, and it is hard to get out. Hard, but not impossible! Imagine you are caught in such a rip current. What is your mind telling you to do in order to survive? For most of us, it's *Swim for shore, kick and stroke to get back onto dry land!* With a rip current, however, this is the worst thing to do. Trying to counter this swift, powerful force will wear you out, allowing it to pull you under. The more you struggle, the more likely you are to drown.

Many of us speak about "battling" or "fighting" cravings. It's like being caught in a rip current—the harder we try to fight the urge to eat unhealthy food, smoke, or use substances, the more the cravings come back. This is also the case with emotions like anxiety, anger, sadness, and grief, which often trigger our cravings. Sometimes no matter how hard we try to fight those feelings, they just seem to get stronger and stronger. It's a back-and-forth struggle with our cravings and with our thoughts and feelings. We're stuck in an exhausting fight for our lives, or so it seems. We may think there's no alternative but to fight. But we do have a choice.

What else could we do? In the case of rip currents, the best thing to do is actually the *opposite* of our natural inclination, or what our minds are telling us to do. In a real rip current, the opposite response is to stay still, float horizontally to increase our surface area, and calmly move out of the current (as shown in the figure). We can deal with cravings in a similar manner. The more we struggle with them, the worse things get and the more helpless we become. However, if we choose to do the opposite of what our minds are telling us, things start to change. This does not mean the craving goes away (the rip current doesn't disappear), but we can get out of the pull of the current and move in our desired direction.

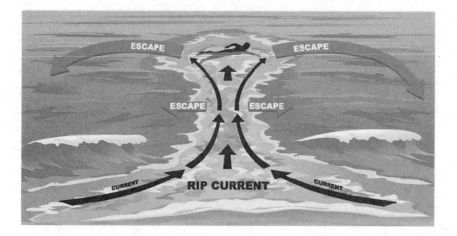

With cravings, we can choose to change our response. We can stop struggling and do the opposite—let go. We can learn to accept these craving experiences for what they are, so we can do what truly matters to us. We can view cravings just like waves breaking on the shore: they come, and they go. Struggling with the waves gets us nowhere. When waves show up, the best response is to wait for them to pass. Yes, they will get us wet, but they will not harm us.

What if we decided to stop trying to get rid of cravings, to instead direct our energy to doing what matters to us? Now we are free to do what we like; we can do something that is important to us. We could connect with a loved one and spend time with them. We could finally use our freedom to accomplish that project we've been waiting to accomplish if only we weren't struggling against the waves. Once we stop trying to get rid of cravings, we notice how much energy and time we've devoted to that struggle. It left us no time to do those things we love.

EXERCISE: Responses to Cravings

Take a moment to observe your thoughts during a craving. What is running through your mind? What would it be like if you allowed yourself to experience any craving thoughts and feelings just as they come, instead of trying to run away from them? In your notebook, make a list of these thoughts.

Let's also consider some common ways we respond to craving-related thoughts using the list below, and then explore what choosing to do the opposite looks like. We urge you to add to this list by addressing your own cravings-related thoughts and considering how you respond whenever you are faced with a difficult situation or catch yourself struggling. Note whether the way you responded was helpful and whether it will help get you to where you want to go. Also consider whether the opposite response would be more appropriate.

You can use your notebook or the Craving Responses worksheet in the online free tools (http://www.newharbinger.com/48336). For example:

Thought: A drink is what I need now.

My common response: I drink to get rid of the cravings.

Opposite response choice: I will recognize that this is just a craving and choose to not drink. I will do something in line with my values—call a loved one.

Which of the responses will work better in this case? Recognizing a craving as just a craving and doing something consistent with my values.

Another example:

Thought: I should not have given in to the craving. I am too weak.

My common response: I will have a cigarette to soothe the guilty feeling.

Opposite response choice: I will acknowledge that quitting smoking is hard—I am only human—but I can choose to not smoke.

Which of the responses will work better in this case? Acknowledging that quitting smoking is hard and choosing not to smoke.

Fai recognized that when she gets stressed out about her job, she thinks about eating sweets to feel better. However, she realized that won't solve the source of her stress, but will only add to it. Thinking of other ways she could approach her challenge, she decided to call her friend to problem solve.

Understanding More About What Triggers Our Cravings

We may be more willing to allow cravings to exist if we learn more about what triggers them, which in turn can help us learn healthier ways to accept and manage them.

There are two different types of triggers (the stimuli that provoke a craving): external and internal.

We often encounter external triggers in our daily lives. These *people-places-things* triggers include seeing other people eating, smoking, and using substances; being in a place where you like to eat, smoke, and use substances; or seeing or smelling what you crave, or things associated with it (for example, watching something enjoyable on TV that you associate with drinking, such as a ball game; smelling tobacco on your clothes; or seeing a recipe for your favorite dessert).

Internal triggers arise within your body. We often use food and substances to change internal states—for instance, to stop experiencing the craving, to feel less stressed, and to distract ourselves from emotions like sadness, anxiety, and anger. We also use substances to avoid withdrawal symptoms.

To find the best strategy for managing these different types of triggers, we must be able to identify them and recognize what we do when they show up.

Take some time now to record your triggers in your notebook or using the Internal and External Triggers Diary, included with the free online tools. The more comprehensive a list you come up with, the better. You'll review this list as you learn more about managing triggers.

Managing External Triggers

When we are learning how to abstain from eating unhealthy food, smoking, drinking, and using drugs, we will likely choose to not be around others when they are engaging in these activities. It may be extremely difficult to resist being in their presence and not using. For instance, Fai might choose not to buy chocolate when she starts making changes to her diet to eat more healthily. Knowing it is in her house could make it hard to resist. Especially at the beginning of your journey to more effectively managing cravings, it's advisable to limit your exposure to the things you crave. Here are some examples of ways to manage your external triggers:

- **Limit exposure to external triggers:** Limit your exposure to people, places, and activities you associate with eating, smoking, or using substances, *particularly* in the first few weeks you are trying to change your approach or abstain.

  Examples: Avoiding other smokers or people using substances; friends you usually use substances with; or favorite places to eat unhealthy food, smoke, drink, or use drugs. Throw out unhealthy food, ashtrays and lighters, and alcohol or drug-related objects.

- **Alter external triggers:** When you cannot easily limit your exposure to external triggers, try changing your routines (choose to do the opposite of your usual).

  Examples: Change your routines first thing in the morning and around mealtimes and after meals; rearrange your furniture or sit in a different place when watching TV; engage in other activities, especially meaningful ones.

- **Use substitutes:** Find appealing replacements for unhealthy food, tobacco, or substances.

  Examples: Try sugarless candies and gum, fruits and veggies, whole-grain baked goods. When you're thirsty, drink water. Replace cigarettes with things that engage your mouth and hands, such as cinnamon sticks, flavored or unflavored toothpicks, straws, worry beads, or stress balls.

However, you may not want to forever avoid restaurants or panic if you run into friends you socialize with by eating unhealthy food, smoking, or using substances. You'll need new strategies to be able to deal with these situations. You can manage these situations by using skills outlined in this book. You must determine what is best for *you* and what you can manage. It may *always* be a good idea to avoid the bakeshop with the irresistible cake, or the pub where you used to drink, or being around friends when they smoke.

Managing Internal Triggers

We can't manage *internal* triggers—like the emotions of anxiety, anger, and sadness, and thoughts about wanting to eat cake, smoke, or use substances—in the same ways we manage external triggers. The same strategies of avoiding and altering may not work. The more we try to not have anxiety, depression, and anger, the more we may experience them (remember the craving control paradox). So we need to use ACT strategies to manage these triggers, which will be the focus of the next few chapters. Rather than trying to control internal triggers, we encourage you to choose to do the opposite, to embrace them and make room for them in your life. Having the thought that you want to have a cigarette does not have to result in your having one. Having anxiety does not mean you must eat to cope with it. Having anger does not mean you need to drink to make it go away. You can have these emotions and still act in service of your values.

You may not have control over whether internal triggers or craving show up, but you do have control over how you respond! Acceptance is an important technique to be able to manage these internal triggers. For instance, Fai might benefit from accepting the cravings she is experiencing, rather than attempting to push them away by eating. Pushing them away just makes them stronger. You'll need additional skills to manage internal triggers. We will turn to these in the next chapter.

Choice Moment Obstacles

You can chart everything we've discussed in this chapter on your Craving Choice Moment Diagram (with the free online tools). Record obstacles that get in the way of your moving toward values-based living (see the figure). At the end of each chapter we'll review the obstacles to values-based living that we discussed in the chapter, as well as the skills that will help us move toward our values when facing a craving choice moment. You will continue to add to your diagram as you build on concepts and learning.

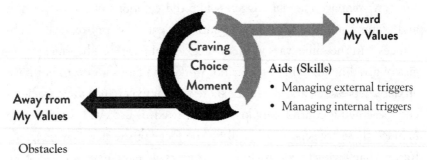

Bringing It All Together

- Craving control paradox: the more we try to control or get rid of cravings, the stronger and more numerous they become.

- Sometimes the best choice is to do the *opposite* of what our mind tells us (rip current metaphor).

- Craving triggers come in two forms: external and internal.

- For external triggers, the best thing to do at the beginning is to *avoid, alter them, or use substitutes.* As we proceed on our behavior change journey, the strategies we discuss in the next few chapters will become useful tools and important techniques for managing internal triggers.

Bringing Our Learning to Life

We suggest that over the next few days, before moving on to the next chapter, you complete the Craving Responses worksheet, available with the online free tools, or complete the list in your notebook.

Also, we encourage you to keep the Internal and External Triggers Diary (found in the online free tools) with you and note when cravings show up and how you manage them. Note whether you fall into your usual patterns of managing the cravings or try the new ideas we explored in this chapter. We emphasized external triggers in this chapter but will talk more about internal triggers in the next chapter. We'll continue discussing the importance and life-changing aspects of being willing to face cravings, thoughts, and feelings, and you will expand your toolbox of skills. We hope these will help you begin to exercise more values-based choices.

CHAPTER 5

Willingness to Make Room for Cravings

Jeff   *The first time I used was in the army. We were bored out of our minds, being on watch for hours on end. Nothing to do, just be there with our minds. It was driving us all crazy. When I got hurt during my deployment, I started taking painkillers. But over time, the painkillers gave me a way out—a way out of my head and a way out from all I was feeling and thinking during the experience of combat. When I returned home from combat, I moved on to heroin. The emotions and thoughts I experienced because of my combat trauma were so overwhelming, they became another version of the enemy for me. They were debilitating me, and all I wanted to do was lose myself in a different world. Then I continued to use, because if I didn't, I would get these monstrous withdrawal symptoms and cravings. I recognize today that my drug use has to do with me wanting to get rid of bothersome thoughts and feelings.*

Jeff's story illustrates how addictive behaviors function as a way to control or escape from unwanted thoughts and feelings. Jeff was trying to control and avoid his thoughts, feelings, and cravings by using drugs. He describes overwhelming thoughts and feelings related to his combat trauma. Of course, if we see our internal world (thoughts, feelings, sensations, cravings) as the enemy, we will fight them. However, as we have discussed, our internal world is there to help and guide us. It is not the enemy! In this chapter we will discuss an alternative to control that helps us stop the useless struggle with our internal experiences and see them not as enemies but as useful guides.

Acting with Willingness: The Antidote to Unwanted Events

On your journey to values-based living, you will inevitably encounter barriers and obstacles. What matters is what you do when faced with these obstacles. (We devote chapter 11 to handling these.) Choosing to recognize and make room for our thoughts, feelings, and bodily sensations is called *willingness*. Willingness means making a choice to see cravings for what they are—thoughts, feelings, sensations, memories—nothing more, no matter what our minds may tell us. Acting with willingness is a choice, wherein you exercise being comfortable with discomfort for the sake of moving forward on your valued-living path. You may not feel motivated all the time—that is normal—yet you can still choose to act with willingness because you want to do something important or meaningful to you.

Acting with willingness involves recognizing what we cannot control (thoughts, emotions, sensations, cravings) and putting our efforts and energy into what we can control (how we talk and behave). For this book's purposes, willingness is not something we possess; it's not a personality characteristic, a feeling or masochistic tendency to subject ourselves to pain. It is also not about liking, tolerating, wanting, approving of, resigning ourself to, or putting up with craving, so that it will go away. Willingness is an action, a behavior we choose to exhibit when craving thoughts and feelings show up because we care about valued, addiction-free living.

EXERCISE: Acting with Willingness in the Face of Cravings

Take a piece of paper. Write down a couple of the values you've identified. On the reverse side, write down the kinds of internal obstacles—craving thoughts, sensations, and feelings—that may show up when you set out on your values-based living journey.

Would you choose to discard this paper if by doing so you would eliminate all chances of having cravings and difficult thoughts and feelings? A tantalizing option, but there's another condition: if you throw all this away, you throw away with it all that you care about.

These are your choices. When we choose to get on a valued-living path, to live with vitality and meaning, we choose to act with willingness and keep both sides of this paper!

What do you choose? Do you choose to continue to spend your life struggling to keep the cravings away, or to live with willingness and courage and take along this piece of paper with both its sides?

If you chose to keep this paper, we suggest that you fold it and keep it in your wallet or another place where you can easily find it. It's a reminder of the choices you have and the costs of these choices. Each time you revisit it, ask yourself how willing you are to have both sides of the paper. At difficult times, take your paper out and look at its two sides. It will help you find that meaning—the willingness—the *why* to keep you going and keep you choosing to live in accordance with your values.

We all act with willingness throughout our daily lives and in a variety of settings. Some days you don't feel like going to work. You may be too tired or unmotivated. Do you still go to work? If you do, you have acted with willingness. You go to work because it matters to you to do a good job, to provide for your family, to have the financial freedom to do things you enjoy. We often face tasks we do not want to do or feel like doing, that won't make us feel particularly good, yet we choose to do them because there is something we care about in doing them. That is acting with willingness. Amy, for example, often described how she hated cooking, especially all the cleaning after the meal is prepared and eaten. Yet she cooked almost every day, because she cared about her children having a warm, healthy home-cooked meal at least once a day. Amy was choosing to act with willingness. In the face of cravings, willingness is choosing to ride the wave and proceeding with a chosen values-driven activity.

A growing body of research supports that acceptance of internal experiences and willingness to act, no matter what we think or feel, make us more functional and satisfied with life; we experience less pain and feel less anxious or depressed (Biglan, Hayes, & Pistorello, 2008; Gloster, Walder, Levin, Twohig, & Karekla, 2020; Vowles & McCracken, 2010). Acting with willingness is not easy; it takes practice. The benefits come from accumulated learning as we persist in values-based actions in the face of difficulties and cravings. Opening up and softening toward our internal world is an act of willingness to experience the cravings; it adds new choices to our behavioral repertoire.

Note: We refer to *acting* with willingness as a choice you make to recognize what you can and cannot control. Your mind may come up with all sorts of horror stories about what may happen if you don't try to control the cravings. Your mind bases these predictions on your past choices. Yet do you truly know what can happen? Have you ever approached your cravings with willingness and openness? You may be surprised to discover, over time, that the predicted dire outcomes don't come to pass. Acting with willingness is a powerful tool that allows you to live a vital and meaningful life.

You'll find an audio version to guide you through the following exercise in the online free tools.

EXERCISE: Putting Willingness into Action

Find a setting where you won't be disturbed, and get seated comfortably. Slowly close your eyes, or find a spot to rest your gaze. Gently guide your attention to your breath. Notice its natural rhythm in your chest and belly. Simply notice the breath without any attempt to make it faster or slower, deeper or shallower. Observe the air coming in and the air coming out.

Slowly imagine going for a nice afternoon walk in a park near a smoothly flowing river. Beautiful sounds and smells are all around you. Take a second to breath all that in. Now stand facing the river. Imagine that this river represents all your *psychological content*—meaning all your thoughts, feelings, sensations, cravings, all the things you have been struggling with.

There are different ways you can have contact with your psychological content. Let's explore some of these.

Sometimes you may get lost in it. This may be like falling into the river and having it carry you away into unknown lands. Experience how it feels to fall into the river and have its currents drag you out into the unknown. It may be easy to do, as you just let yourself go and let the river carry you...Yet it can be pretty scary, as you may find yourself in places you did not really want to go. And each time you fall in and get pulled somewhere, you have to find your way back. This can become exhausting. Notice how all this feels. Now compare this to the way you may let your cravings, feelings, and thoughts carry you wherever they want. This is not willingness or acceptance; this is resigning, surrendering.

Another way to have contact with psychological content is by struggling to stop it or get rid of it. Imagine that you find yourself again in the river. This time you stand firmly in the water, trying to block it, trying to not let the water flow and not let it sweep you away. How does that feel? This may also be tiring, exhausting...if you ease up for even a second, you get pulled off your feet. Notice how your body feels with this approach to your psychological content. Notice how your breath changes to accommodate this, and how stiff and tense your muscles feel. Compare this with how you may struggle to resist cravings and how it may feel like hours and hours of manual work without a break.

However, there is another way of being in contact with your psychological content—your feelings, thoughts and cravings—without struggling or being carried away. Imagine that you now sit on a pier. You take off your shoes and socks and gently lower your feet into this cool river water. Notice the feeling of the cool water running against your feet, and notice how you can now feel this water without trying to change it in any way. The water may feel a bit cold at first; you slowly get used to it. Now observe your body, your breath, and your muscles. In this position your hands are free to do whatever they want, and you can watch the birds flying up above, listen to the sounds around you, smell the scents of the water and the land, and feel the sensations of changing temperatures on your skin. Acting with willingness in the face of cravings and associated thoughts and feelings is like sitting on the pier and choosing to stick your feet into the cool water. This may be very different from what your mind has been telling you.

At times your old ways of approaching your psychological content may reappear, and you may find yourself back to fighting with the river current or being carried away by it. When this happens, remember you now have a new way: you can choose to come out of the water, and sit on the pier, and willingly place your feet in the water.

Take a moment to experience this new way of contacting your psychological content. When you are ready, slowly open your eyes and rejoin the setting where your visualization began.

This exercise may be a bit challenging at first, since you may not have had much experience of opening up to your psychological content and cravings. You may feel different things each time. One time relaxed, another time tense; sometimes you may be able to sit for a long time on the pier, at others times you may keep falling into the water and struggling. All of these are perfectly fine. With practice, it will become easier to act with willingness and gently open up to your cravings.

Facing Cravings

Willingness to experience your cravings is the key to changing your addictive behaviors and your relationships with the substance(s) you've used. In the ACT approach we have been following throughout this book, it is important to acknowledge that you will find yourself yourself in situations where it is likely that cravings will show up; these are the times to use all the tools in this book.

When we first start making changes in how we approach cravings, it helps to practice getting used to having cravings. That may sound funny, but when we know that we are not going in give in to our cravings anymore, we have to become used to just having them. And it's okay to have cravings! We all have them in some form or another. We might as well make room for them and, if possible, even make friends with them.

We encourage you to try the following facing cravings exercise before you decide to quit using any substance. For substance use—smoking, drinking, and using drugs—once you commit to abstinence, it is important to ensure that you refrain from smoking, drinking, or using drugs altogether. Purposefully putting yourself in the face of cravings in the early recovery stage can be particularly difficult, so we don't recommend that. But it is important to learn how to become comfortable with having cravings, and that is often best done before committing to giving up a particular substance. When it comes to food (this cannot work for other substances or alcohol), you have the choice of consuming a small amount rather than refraining from eating the desired foods altogether. The point of this exercise is to practice acting with willingness no matter what the mind and body produce, or how intense the craving is, and to start having experiences in which you make values-based choices.

The next exercise is an aid for willingly facing cravings. Facing cravings will not make them go away, but it will make them more manageable, since you can use your new tools when cravings show up.

EXERCISE: Facing Cravings

Start by finding a comfortable position in which you can sit undisturbed. Close your eyes and bring your attention to your breath.

Focus on each gentle inhale and exhale, noticing the natural rhythm of your chest rising and falling. As you follow the soft flow of your breath, imagine a craving forming. It shows up like an old acquaintance. If it is hard to bring up the sensation, you can recall a time when you felt this craving. Take a second to notice what happens within you when this craving appears. Notice the changes in your body, your breath, your muscles, and your skin. Continue to breathe as you notice these changes. Let yourself notice the craving. Acknowledge its presence and breathe with it.

Where does it appear? Is it within or outside of you? What shape does it have? What color? Temperature? Where does it start and where does it end? See if you can hold it with your mind, as you would hold a soft toy. Gently stroke it as if you were petting your favorite animal. Notice it changing as you hold and caress it. Also, notice your own reactions changing as you change the way you interact with it. Continue to look at it, explore it, and warmly hold and stroke it. You are willingly acting to interact with your craving in a different way because you want to live a life based on what matters to you, not what the craving demands of you. You may notice that its demands change as you hold it, accept it, and make room for it. Holding your craving as gently as you would hold a fragile glass vase.

As you continue to caress this craving, be aware that cravings, like all other feelings and thoughts, are important; they serve or have served a purpose in the past. Ask yourself whether you can make room for this orphaned, unwanted feeling. It does not have to be the enemy. You can choose to see it for what it is—a bunch of sensations, feelings, and thoughts. Even if your mind is telling you that you should not have it, are you willing to open up a space within you for it? Search inside and find a place where you can make a home for this craving. Build its imaginary home and place it inside. Communicate to it that it now has a home where it can stay; no more fighting to get rid of it. Acknowledge that it may visit you from time to time and that you will willingly act to let it be there while you continue to live your life with purpose and vitality.

Allow yourself to experience this new way of interacting with your craving, then slowly return to noticing your body, your muscles, your breathing. Notice that as you were doing this exercise, you rode the craving wave. Slowly return to your breath and yourself in the room and open your eyes.

How was this exercise for you? Were you able to contact your craving in a different way? Did you make some room for the craving to exist within you?

As you practice this exercise, you will start to increase your self-control over your actions. You will also struggle less, so you may feel less tired, drained, and powerless.

Choice Moment Aids

This chapter discussed willingness and acceptance of internal events or things that are out of our control, thus allowing us to focus our efforts and energy on doing things that matter based on our values. In the following figure we present a craving choice moment as the point when we can choose which direction to take—move toward our values or away from them. (If you haven't already begun using a blank diagram from the online free tools, download one now so you can start to write your personal obstacles and aids.)

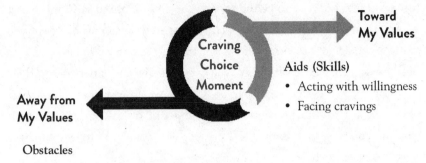

Bringing It All Together

- Willingness is the process of actively making room for all internal events and cravings and choosing to act in accordance with your values.

- Acting with willingness is the antidote to struggling with things we cannot control (thoughts, emotions, sensations).

- All the psychological content we struggle with stems from having important things we care about in life.

- Facing our cravings and accepting them—while acting with willingness based on our values—paradoxically helps to free us from cravings and allows us to focus on the kind of life we want to live.

Bringing Our Learning to Life

Try practicing this chapter's exercises. The more you practice, the more you'll gain. Practice with willingness even if your mind produces excuses or the exercise is challenging. Throughout your day, when you notice that you are struggling with your psychological content—your thoughts, feelings, or cravings—practice changing the way you respond to it. Willingly make room for your cravings and respond in ways that give you a sense of purpose and vitality.

In the next chapter, we will discover how taking a step back from our cravings can help free us to make decisions based on what is important to us.

CHAPTER 6

Taking a Step Back from Your Cravings

Fai *I always had difficulty managing my cravings. When I am really stressed, I think about eating chocolate and believe that it will bring me comfort. I think, I'm so stressed that I really need chocolate right now to feel better. It's hard to get these thoughts out of my mind. I try to push them away, but they just come back, and they are often even stronger than when the craving first started. I get so tired of trying to push them away that I just give in and binge on chocolate. Afterward, I always feel bad about myself and berate myself for not having more "willpower." I believe that I can only stop eating chocolate if I can get rid of my cravings and my stressful thoughts. But I realize that this hasn't been working for me, and I can't make all of my cravings and stressful thoughts go away. I wonder if there is another way to manage them.*

We humans are an amazing species. Our ability to think and plan has resulted in the creation of fantastic things! This is why humans have been so successful—we can plan ahead and anticipate problems, communicate with others, and problem solve. We have developed complex cultures and civilizations. Our ability to think and plan has culminated in people walking on the moon and sophisticated data-gathering devices on distant planets! However, there is also a downside to our amazing thinking abilities: sometimes we are so busy thinking and preoccupied with our thoughts that we get lost in them. We are often not living in the present, but thinking about the past or worrying about the future. We are constantly thinking and reacting to our thoughts.

Cravings are part of this picture. Sometimes we get so focused on cravings that we can't think of anything else. And like Fai, we fight those cravings, trying to push them away. But inevitably, it takes so much energy to fight them that we just give in. But any relief is short lived, and next time they may be stronger than ever.

Remember the tiger that represented our cravings in chapter 2? When you feed the tiger it just gets bigger, hungrier, and scarier. One day, you walk to your fridge and there's no more meat left to give; there's nothing left to feed it but yourself! If we use substances every time we have an urge to, we're feeding the tiger, and it keeps coming back for more. What is the only way to get the tiger to leave? To stop feeding it. The only way to effectively manage cravings is to stop feeding them too.

Think about who's running your life. Is it your cravings or you? Who's in control here? You don't have to devote your life or lose your life to this tiger. You can stop feeding the tiger by using mindful acceptance and compassion for yourself (more on these concepts in chapter 8).

Why do cravings feel so powerful and hard to resist? The thought *I need a drink* can be as difficult to ignore as the tiger. Let's explore how these thoughts get to be so powerful in the first place.

EXERCISE: Milk, Milk, Milk
(Hayes, Strosahl, & Wilson, 1999)

We're going to ask you to do something silly. We (Maria and Megan) usually do this exercise with our clients—so we're happy to participate with you!

Say the word "milk" out loud. What comes to your mind when you think of milk? The usual associations: it is a liquid, you drink it, it's white, it comes from animals (cows, goats), it's sold in a bottle or carton. As you think of the word "milk" you may actually "see" some of these images—a glass of milk, a carton of milk, a cow or goat. You may even taste it in your mouth. Interesting! These things are not physically present, but they are psychologically present. We heard a sound inside our head or read some characters grouped on a piece of paper—m-i-l-k—and then all those pictures, memories, and thoughts showed up.

Now, try repeating the word "milk" over and over again for thirty to sixty seconds. *Milk, milk, milk, milk, milk, milk*...repeat it faster and faster. What happens when you do this? Has the word become just a strange, funny sound? Has the word lost its psychological links (the mental pictures)? Well, after about thirty seconds of repeating any word it will start to sound really strange. It loses its meaning. We don't think about that glass of milk anymore—all we are left with is a sound. However, we don't usually think of milk this way—it usually symbolizes something. But ultimately it is just a word. Four letters that were put together and associated with the creamy white liquid we have learned to call "milk."

What if now we asked you to think of the word "γάλα"? What would show up? You would probably think *What are these weird characters? This seems like Greek to me!* And it *is* Greek. It is the Greek word for "milk." If you do not speak or read Greek, this word will have no meaning for you, whereas if you speak Greek (as Maria does), you'll evoke the same images and sensations that showed up with "milk." So the word has meaning because we have attributed meaning to it. Words are not solid or tangible. They are more like the blowing wind; they come and go.

Now let's think about your cravings. Consider the thought *I need a drink, a smoke, or chocolate.* This thought just a bunch of words, too, aside from the meaning we give them. Let's repeat the milk exercise with one word for the craving substance you may struggle with (chocolate, cigarettes, alcohol, pot, and so on). What images and sensations come to mind when you think of this craving word? Maybe different experiences you've had with what the word represents? Again, all you did was think of that word.

Now repeat the word out loud over and over for the next thirty to sixty seconds. Say it faster and faster.

What happened? Did the word end up being just a strange sound? Did it lose its meaning?

Try repeating this exercise when you have a craving and see what happens to your craving. Megan had a client who used this exercise to help himself overcome his urges to smoke. Whenever he had an urge to smoke, instead of trying to push that thought away, he would repeat to himself, "smoke, smoke, smoke, smoke, smoke." After about thirty seconds the word no longer had any meaning for him and he went about his day. He found this technique particularly helpful for taking the power out of his cravings to smoke. You can do this with other words that make you feel uncomfortable, like *anxious*, *scared*, and *angry*. If you repeat them over and over, you will start to see the meaning disappear. This can also help you manage your cravings, because strong emotions are often linked to cravings. This exercise is not intended to make the cravings disappear, but to change how you relate to the cravings.

We have no control over the emergence of our feelings and thoughts—they are just the result of our experiences and our present circumstances. However, we do have control over whether we act on our thoughts and feelings. Our thoughts and feelings do not necessarily have to lead to action. For example, you have probably had a day when you thought how nice it would be to not show up for work, yet you probably went to work anyway. When we realize that we don't always have to act on every thought and feeling, that we can choose whether we act on our cravings, we can practice acceptance of our cravings and other thoughts and feelings. We can let go of feeling the need to avoid these experiences. The thought *I need a drink* isn't very different from any other thought that we have. We are free to choose whether to act on our cravings, thoughts, and feelings. We can choose to act on them or on what is meaningful to us.

You Don't Need Any Substance to Cope with Stress

Thoughts, feelings, and cravings are normal responses to life events. It is impossible to get rid of all stress, anxiety, sadness, and anger. We often think an emotion like anxiety is a terrible thing. Emotions like anxiety are often labeled as "negative emotions." However, these emotions are normal reactions to the challenges of life. It's good to have some level of stress, anxiety, and anger in our lives—they help us to achieve our goals. Imagine if we didn't have any anxiety at all. How would that help or harm us? For instance, if we were going for a job interview and we didn't experience any related stress or anxiety, what would happen? We might not prepare for the interview. We might even show up in sneakers and sweatpants. Then we might not be evaluated well and not get the job. Some level of stress or anxiety helps ensure we will prepare, to increase our chances of securing the job, as it is part of the values-based life we want. But what if we have too much stress or anxiety? That's not good either—we may not even show up for the interview. So we strive for a good balance of emotions in our lives—not too little and not too much. *You don't want to be rid of any emotion—you just want a good, healthy balance.* This figure illustrates the point. Optimal performance is supported by a stress level that is neither too low nor too high.

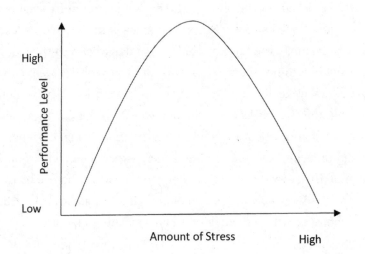

EXERCISE: When Have Emotions Been Helpful?

Think about times in your life when different emotions—anxiety, sadness, and anger—have actually been helpful. Record these in your notebook. After some reflection, can you see that anxiety, anger, or sadness don't always have to be "bad" experiences?

Accepting our thoughts and feelings, even when they are uncomfortable, is often necessary and helpful. If we avoid unwanted thoughts and emotions as a coping strategy—particularly when we avoid by using a substance—we might feel good temporarily, but in the long run the avoidance is really harming us. Again, we don't always have to act on our thoughts and feelings. By accepting them as normal thoughts and feelings that are even helpful in a lot of situations, we gain more power over them.

Here's another example to demonstrate the struggle with our feelings and thoughts (Hayes et al., 1999). Imagine driving your car to an important destination. Think of this destination as one of your values-driven goals outlined in chapter 3. You have passengers—two small children in the back seat. These children don't want to go where you're headed. They want to go to the toy store or the candy store. They throw a tantrum and scream to try to get their way. What do you do? This is a choice moment! You have a choice—you are the driver. You can give in to the howling kids, or you can continue to the important destination. You might want to give in and take them where *they* want to go, to make them stop causing such a ruckus. But what happens then? They may quiet down for a little while, but soon enough they will start right up again. Remember, you are the driver. Can you still get to your destination despite the tantrums? Yes, you can. And eventually, when the kids realize that you don't give in to them, they will settle down. It's the same with cravings. Your cravings will scream and rage, and if you give in to them they may calm down for a while, but they will be back. The more you give in to them, the worse they get. You have a choice—you are the driver here. If you don't give in to cravings, they may throw a tantrum for a while, but inevitably they will calm down. This doesn't mean they ever really go away, but they may be less intense and more manageable.

You always have a choice as to whether you give in to the cravings—they do not have to control you.

Don't Believe Everything Your Mind Tells You

Your mind tells you all sorts of things. If you have cravings, your mind may tell you, *If I don't use, I am going to go crazy!* or *If I don't smoke, I won't be able to handle this!* But you don't always have to believe it!

Your mind is like a good buddy of yours—he's looking out for you. He'll alert you to dangers in your life—like if there's a fire, he'll tell you to get out of the house. If there's a car coming in your direction, your buddy pushes you out of the way. It's really helpful to have a friend who is keeping you safe, just like a good friend should. But your friend can also be a little skittish. For instance, if you hear a loud bang in the kitchen, your friend may tell you it's an intruder when it's actually just a cat pushing a pot off the counter. Your buddy may think those were gunshots when it was just a car backfiring. Now, you definitely think the friend is helpful—he has told you about some significant dangers. However, your friend has been wrong too. Your mind produces thoughts that are helpful and some that are not. You don't have to believe everything your mind tells you. Your mind might tell you that if you don't use drugs or alcohol, if you don't eat that chocolate or smoke that cigarette, you may go crazy. But that thought is not helpful. When we have cravings and think that something terrible is going to happen if we don't give in to them, we need to take a step back from the situation and see whether our minds, our good buddies, are telling us the truth or just sounding another false alarm. We call this stepping-back technique *cognitive defusion*.

EXERCISES THAT CAN HELP

Let's go over some exercises that can help you to take a step back or defuse from your cravings and other thoughts and emotions.

EXERCISE #1: *I am having the thought…***or** *I am having the feeling…*
(Hayes, 2005)

When we have a craving, we often say to ourselves *I need a drink* or *I need some ice cream*. It may feel like we "need" this substance, but is this craving actually more of a "want"? Try prefacing the thought with *I am having the thought that*. So instead of *I need a drink* you can say to yourself, *I am having the thought that I need a drink*. Instead of *I need ice cream*, you can say *I am having the thought that I need ice cream*. Notice the difference it makes. It can help to give you a little bit of space between your thought and how you react to it—some breathing room to make a choice based on what is truly important to you. You can also do this for other thoughts and feelings that you have that might trigger a craving. For instance, you may have the thought *I am sad*. You can even use that thought as a reason for not doing things that may be important to you. But can you still feel sad and do what's important to you? Yes! Try beginning the thought with *I am having the feeling that...* Now the thought becomes *I am having the feeling that I am sad.* This acknowledges that you are feeling sad, but you are not sadness. You may be experiencing sadness, but you do not need to be defined by it, and it does not need to make your life choices for you.

See if adding these phrases to your thoughts gives you a little room between them and the choices you make. It may make the difference between giving in to a craving or doing something healthier like taking a walk or talking to a friend.

EXERCISE #2: Thank Your Mind for Your Thoughts

In this exercise, you thank your mind for your thoughts, as you would thank a friend for their advice. You can even give your mind a name, if you want! You can thank your mind for the craving that you experience, recognizing that this craving is not you, but a thought your mind is generating. You're not ridiculing your mind for coming up with difficult thoughts, like cravings; rather, you're gently acknowledging your thoughts with compassion and then focusing your attention on what is important to you. So *Thank you, mind, for the thought that I need a cigarette right now.* Once you say this, you are back in control of driving the car and having a choice as to where to head to.

EXERCISE #3: Think of Your Cravings as a Bossy Person

When you have a craving, think of that thought as a bossy person pushing you around. Ask yourself: *Who is actually in charge here?* Is your craving in charge, or are you in charge? Think about how you might respond to someone who is pushing you around the way your craving is. Can you stand up for yourself and tell that thought that you're in charge and you'll make the decisions here? It helps to separate your thought from yourself and decide what you want your life to look like.

EXERCISE #4: Leaves on a Stream (Hayes, 2005)

This is one of the most popular exercises among the people we (Megan and Maria) work with. It is best done with closed eyes and as a mindfulness exercise (you can record it yourself, or download a recording from the online free tools at http://www.newharbinger.com/48336).

1.   Seat yourself comfortably where you won't be disturbed. Sit upright
     with your feet flat on the floor, your arms and legs uncrossed, your
     hands resting in your lap.

2.   Allow your eyes to close, or choose a spot on the ground a few feet in
     front of you and let your gaze go slightly out of focus.

3.   Take a few moments to get in touch with the physical sensations in your
     body, especially where your body makes contact with the chair, also
     noticing where your soles touch the floor.

4.   As you continue to notice the physical sensations in your body, also
     start to notice your breathing. Allow a breathing pace that's comfort-
     able for you. Notice yourself breathing in and breathing out.

5.   It's okay for your mind to wander to thoughts, worries, images, bodily
     sensations, or feelings. Just notice these and acknowledge their pres-
     ence. Observe the flow of your thoughts, one after the other, without
     trying to figure out their meaning. As best as you can, bring an atti-
     tude of gentle acceptance to your experience in the present moment—
     the here and now. Simply allow your experience without trying to
     change it.

6.   Now imagine it's a nice fall afternoon. Walking in the park, you come
     across a quiet glade near a stream. You decide to sit down for a few
     minutes next to the stream. You notice a number of colorful leaves
     have fallen on the surface of the water. Watch the leaves slowly drift
     downstream. As you watch, more leaves may fall onto the water and
     drift away.

7.   For the next few moments, when thoughts come along, put each one
     on a leaf. Observe as each leaf comes closer to you, then watch it
     slowly drift away, eventually drifting out of sight. Return to gazing at
     the stream, waiting for the next leaf to float by with a new thought.

8.   When one comes along, again watch it come closer, then let it drift
     away. Think whatever thoughts you think and allow them to flow freely,
     each on a leaf, one by one. Your thoughts float by on the leaves. No

need to run after each of them or to push them away yourself. Just notice them come and go. As soon as one goes, another one probably just shows up. Notice how some thoughts/leaves may come in groups and how they again appear and slowly drift away.

9. When you are ready, see if you can let go of those thoughts and become aware again of your breathing—the in-breath and out-breath, at whatever pace is comfortable for you. Gradually widen your attention to take in the sounds around you in the room. When you're ready, open your eyes and bring your attention back to the room.

It's good to check in with yourself after this mindfulness exercise. What did you notice in these few minutes? This exercise can help you to experience that you are separate from your thoughts and feelings. It can also introduce some distance between you and your thoughts. When you create distance between yourself and your thoughts, you stop struggling with them; it can empower you to choose which thoughts you want to act on. A craving may be here now, but it will pass, just like your other thoughts. Notice that every time a thought, a craving, or a feeling shows up, it is a choice moment: you can choose how to act. The choice is not of how you are thinking or feeling but how you want to *act* even if these thoughts and feelings are present. Try to make choices based on what matters to you, not transitory cravings, thoughts, or emotions. You will find you are much more satisfied with your life, and the cravings will not have control over you.

EXERCISE #5: Urge Surfing

Another really helpful exercise for managing cravings is urge surfing. Tons of research demonstrates that cravings last only a few minutes—they peak like an ocean wave and then break. Sometimes cravings *feel* like they last forever. Similarly, it may feel like a lifetime passes in the time it takes for a high ocean wave to hit you and pass, but waves and cravings really only last a few minutes. Can you wait out the craving? Try this exercise when you have a craving.

As you experience the craving, bring yourself back to the awareness of your breath. Imagine your breath as a surfboard that can help you to ride out the craving. Notice any physical sensations, such as sweating or tense muscles. Notice your feelings: do you feel anxious or on edge? Notice any thoughts, like *I need to smoke, I need a drink, I can't handle this, I want this to go away*. Watch as these sensations, feelings, and thoughts rise, peak, and eventually subside. Imagine yourself surfing the wave of the sensations associated with your craving. Practice riding your sensations, feelings, and thoughts on your surfboard until they lessen and disappear. Use your breath as a vehicle to ride out these experiences and bring you back to the present moment until the craving passes.

Choice Moment Aids

In this chapter we discovered a new skill—cognitive defusion—and exercises we can use as aids to help us in the face of obstacles to values-based living, as this figure illustrates. We will build on these skills in the coming chapters. You can add your favorite aids to your Craving Choice Moment Diagram (see the online free tools, http://www.newharbinger.com/48336) and build your library of skills as we journey together.

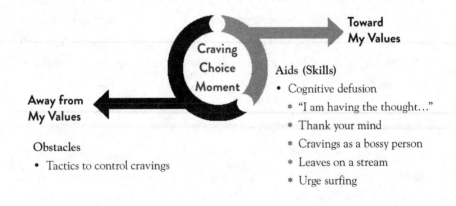

Bringing It All Together

- Humans' ability to think and plan has resulted in great achievements for ourselves and our societies. However, this amazing ability also means we often get stuck in our own minds, thinking about cravings, what happened in the past and what might happen in the future, and we're not often in the here and now.

- You can break free from your cravings by taking a step back from them, cognitively defusing, and realizing that your cravings are separate from you. You then have a choice moment, in which you can choose whether you want to listen to your cravings or focus on what is important to you.

- You can do the same with thoughts and feelings that often trigger cravings: you can choose whether you want them to make decisions for you, or if you'd rather focus on what matters to you.

- Try some exercises that help you to take a step back and cognitively defuse from your cravings and other thoughts and feelings. Thank your mind for your thoughts. Use the phrase *I am having the thought that...*or *I am having the feeling that...*before your thoughts, and practice the Leaves on the Stream or Urge Surfing exercises to introduce some space between yourself and your cravings and other thoughts and feelings. These exercises can give you a little room to decide whether you want cravings to make decisions for you or you would like to make those choices yourself.

Bringing Our Learning to Life

Give these exercises a try over the next week and see if they reduce the intensity of your cravings. Identify which exercises work best for you and add them to your daily practice.

In the next chapter, we will expand on the idea of the self being separate from thoughts and feelings.

CHAPTER 7

Separating Ourselves from Cravings

Kap *Who am I? I am a smoker. That is who I am. I am this incapable person who knows he should not be smoking yet he still does. I am this helpless person who is unable to stop these cravings and gives in to smoking each time. I am this idiot who keeps failing at giving up smoking. I am an embarrassment. I do not like who I am! I wish I was stronger, with more willpower and the ability to withstand these cravings.*

This is the response Kap provided when Maria asked him "Who are you?" during one of their first sessions.

Before you read further, take a minute to answer this question for yourself. In your notebook, write your responses to the question "Who am I?" Write as many answers as come to mind.

When Maria asked Kap who he is, he gave her a story related to his smoking, his cravings, and his struggle to quit smoking on his own. We all tend to do that—provide stories about the things we struggle with, areas where we may have fallen short, and sometimes about our personal qualities that we like. What did you write? What stories do you tell yourself about yourself? Notice that we are calling our responses to the question of who we are "stories."

The Stories We Tell Ourselves About Who We Are

Stories are collections of words we create about ourselves. They involve judgments, evaluations, thoughts, images, memories, feelings, somatic sensations, impulses, roles we adopt, and rules we come up with that usually guide how we navigate our world. We tend to think these stories comprise who we are—what we might call our "identity."

Some stories may be benign and may even make us proud of being something we aspired to be (such as "I am a good friend," "I am a dependable professional"). However, many of this story may lead us into problems. Many may buy into the myths we discussed in chapter 1. Take, for example, the story Kap was telling about himself in the opening of this chapter: "I am helpless and incapable." Kap has constructed a story that in order to be considered a capable and strong person he should not have any cravings. This makes it sound like until cravings go away, Kap will be generally helpless and incapable (you may recognize the problem with "I should be able to control cravings"; we've learned that no one is capable of achieving craving control). If Kap adopts this story as being who he is and weaves it into his identity, he may feel helpless and incapable in other areas of life—his relationships, his professional life, and so on. Further, buying into such stories has been shown to lead to *self-stigma*, whereby a person buys into attitudes that they are different from others, morally weak, incompetent, unreliable, deceitful, and so on. This is further associated with *shame*, which can in turn lead the person to perceive themselves as flawed in both their own eyes and others'. They then experience additional feelings of inferiority and self-blame, which are associated with diminished self-esteem, increased mental health symptoms, avoidance of or delay in seeking treatment, disconnect from meaningful social relationships, and lower quality of life (Luoma & Kohlenberg, 2012). Interestingly, people who experience a lot of shame are perceived to focus so much on what is going on for them internally that they seem arrogant and self-centered and show a lack of empathy or awareness of others' feelings. This additionally impacts the quality of their social interactions and can even lead to further use of substances as a way to cope with the whole whirlpool of negative judgments and outcomes. This looks very much like the rip currents we mentioned in chapter 4: once the person is caught up in them, it is hard to get out if they continue to fight the current—to fight with the stories, thoughts, and emotions.

Take a second now to consider the stories you tell about yourself:

1. Are you this story all of the time, in every place and situation? For example, is Kap incapable at his job, at his relationships with friends and loved ones? Like many of us, Kap would respond that he is not. When actually asked this, he said he knows he is capable of many things, and the "incapability" refers mainly to his inability to fight his cravings. It does seem like the stories our minds make up may not be true of all aspects of our lives. Maybe, just as Kap's story does not accurately reflect who Kap is, our own stories don't fully reflect who we are.

2. Who would you be if you got rid of your stories? Surprisingly, Kap responded to this by saying that he would be able to stop struggling with the cravings and give up smoking.

The problem with the stories we tell about ourselves is that they *seem* true, so we need to behave in accordance with them and not behave in a way inconsistent with them. Our stories say things like "I am [insert your story here], so I cannot [insert what valued action you are not doing here]." Note in your notebook what your stories say about you.

Interestingly, no matter what the mind says or the story is about, we have a choice as to how to behave. Let's test this with a silly little exercise.

Remember the Simon Says game you may have played as a kid? Let's play it together, but with a twist. In this variation, we want you to do the *opposite* of what Simon says. So Simon will tell you one thing to do, and you have to do the opposite of what he says. Ready?

- Simon says, "Do not clap your hands." Go ahead, do the opposite. Now, can you say this direction out loud and at the same time do the opposite?

- Simon says, "Lift your left arm up." Go ahead; see if you can do the opposite of lifting your left arm up.

- Simon says, "Do not smile."

What happened? Were you able to read and hear Simon's direction, yet do the opposite? It may seem harder to do the opposite of the direction given, especially since you may have played this game differently many times, yet it is not impossible. And we can say one thing while doing another. Right? How many times have you said something like "I will not give in to this craving" and then given in to it? Again, we do not have to behave how our mind tells us to or go along with whatever story our mind creates about us.

The Illusion of Stories

Actually, stories may be much like the optical illusion shown here. As you stare at it, it seems to quiver. Yet this is a static picture. The movement is created by your mind. There is a whole science behind how such illusions are created, but the point is to recognize that this movement is created solely in your mind, just like the stories your mind tells about you and who you are. The stories of who we are, are merely constructions of our minds! Just as the movement in the optical illusion is not real, these stories are not true all the time or in all contexts. Recognizing this can help us connect to who we are. We are not just one thought, one adjective. We are a lot more than that.

Let's do another exercise to experience what we mean. This exercise is best done while listening, rather than reading, so you can have your eyes closed. You can record it yourself or use the recording with the online free tools (http://www.newharbinger.com/48336).

EXERCISE: Sky Exercise
(inspired by Harris, 2009, and Joanne Dahl)

I (Maria) remember as a child how I loved summer nights when we would go to the beach and lie on the sand and just watch the starry sky. I invite you to imagine such a scene, where you and I lie on a warm blanket on the soft sand, smelling the soft sea breeze, and for a few minutes we look up and enjoy the spectacular starlit sky. Watch this night sky and examine with curiosity and awe the immense sea of stars, larger and smaller, brighter and duller, closer and farther away...an amazing show of lights. Notice, also, closer than the stars may be the kind of clouds you can see at night. For a moment now, let's focus our attention on one of these stars and stare at it, keeping our gaze fixed on this star...and notice what happens. This little star may start to flicker, blink, or even disappear and then come back again. Let's do the same with a cloud. Choose a cloud and observe its whiteness or grayness against the black sky. Watch it for a few moments, as if you are trying to make out a shape. We may make out the shape of a face, then we may notice it changing and morphing into something else, with another shape emerging. As we keep looking, we see that these clouds continuously change; some gather together, others drift apart. The only certain thing about the night sky with its stars and clouds is that it continuously changes.

It is the same with our thoughts, our feelings, and our cravings. They come and they go like the stars and the clouds, constantly changing. Yet you are like the black sky. The infinite, indestructible, black night sky. The sky is not threatened by changes in the weather and the positioning of the stars. The black sky is constant, however the weather changes, no matter how dreadful it sometimes gets. The black sky is always there, whether the clouds are white and fluffy, or dark and full of rain, lightning, and thunder. You are like the black sky. You are neither threatened nor made helpless by changes in your thoughts, feelings, or cravings. These are just content—the stories your mind tells—and they just come and go, rise and fall. *You* are always *greater than* anything you feel, think, or sense.

Connect with your black sky vastness, knowing that *you are always greater than* any thought, feeling, craving, or story. Connect with the idea that the weather will always change, and no matter how bad it gets, whether there is the most severe blizzard or the loudest thunderstorm, nothing can harm the sky. Sometimes we forget the sky is there, yet it is! The sky is there whether we can see it or it's hiding behind the clouds. The sky may be obscured for a little while, but it is always there behind the thunderclouds, stretching into the universe, infinite, limitless. So the next time you feel overwhelmed by a craving, a thought, or a feeling, come back to the black sky and remember *who you are.*

This exercise is meant to give you a different perspective, one where you can start to experience yourself as separate from your stories, as you are separate from the clothes you wear or the furniture you sit on. Yes, it's easier to separate ourselves from these external accessories than from our psychological content. Yet you can experience the difference between yourself and your internal private events (thoughts, memories, feelings, sensations, cravings) to loosen your grip on or attachment to them. By practicing, you can start to access this different perspective of looking at your internal world. You will be able to contact what we call a "safe space" within you, a space that resembles the black sky, where you have room and are open to any difficult thoughts, feelings, or cravings. You also gain the "enduring you" perspective, from which you can observe these internal events without trying to control or change them, without struggling with them or clinging to them. In the ACT approach offered in this book, we delineate a part of ourselves that *observes* and one that *experiences* our world (both internal and external worlds). These parts are distinct from our thoughts, feelings, memories, impulses, physical sensations, and cravings.

Observing and Experiencing Self

To illustrate an observing versus an experiencing self, consider some areas of your life. Recall the last time you felt angry. Recall any bodily sensations—maybe a slight increase in your temperature or a change in your breathing. Notice that a part of you experienced those feelings and another part observed them.

Now consider your thoughts. See if you can be aware of what is going on in your mind right now. Notice anything that your mind is producing at this moment. Notice that you are capable of noticing. A part of you is experiencing those thoughts and another part is observing.

Yet you are not just the emotions you felt last time you were angry or the thoughts passing through your mind now. You are more than that!

Let's try this with cravings. Bring to mind a situation associated with cravings for you. In this situation you immediately feel a longing for the substance associated with the craving. Notice both the physical and emotional needs. Describe the place, the room, the people present, the sounds and smells. Notice what changes in your body—breathing changes, muscle tension, increased heartbeat. Acknowledge that you are also noticing these changes. Recognize that you are not just your craving thoughts, sensations, and feelings. You are more than that! Acknowledge, that across time, your thoughts, sensations, feelings, knowledge, stories, and roles have all been changing—possibly even as you were reading this book. Yet despite changes in all these internal events, there is always a part of you—stable, consistently aware, observing, enduring—that holds all these events while also being separate from them. It is the you that has been there your entire life!

By contacting the observer part of yourself, you will start to experience that you are bigger than any craving, urge, thought, or emotion you struggle with. This observer part, your enduring self, is not and cannot be damaged by any of these experiences.

Now consider the following questions and write answers in your notebook.

- How are you experiencing your cravings at this moment?

- How would you describe your relationship to your cravings now, compared to before reading this chapter?

- Any thoughts about the cravings?

- What are your conclusions regarding your experience of engaging with the content of this chapter?

As you answer these questions, we hope you may start to notice changes in the relationship between *yourself* and your craving experiences (thoughts, emotions, sensations). If you do not notice such changes yet, we suggest you close the book and give yourself some time to consider this new perspective. After a day or so, reread this chapter, listen to the exercises, and reconsider your relationship with your cravings. As you start to recognize and connect with the observer part of yourself and experience yourself as the sky, your relationship to all the cravings, urges, thoughts, emotions, and stories you've been struggling with changes, giving you a fresh perspective.

New Perspective and New Valued Steps

With your new perspective, what steps would you like to take today that you may have been avoiding due to cravings or the fear that cravings will show up? What steps can you take toward the values-based life you want to live? What is something difficult that you choose to do today in line with your values?

Imagine taking a step in this direction, starting with this chosen action. Slowly notice what happens. You may start to experience a movement within you. Your body may start to become activated (breathing changing, heartbeat quickening); your mind may produce warning thoughts (*You will fail, You cannot stand to feel this emotion*) or old stories (*You are incapable of achieving anything; this is no different*). You may experience other emotions (fear, anxiety, confusion). And in that moment when all this shows up, *you have a choice!* This is a choice moment. Will you stop?

Or will you acknowledge all these "clouds," find your "sky" perspective, and choose to take the next step, taking along with you all your clouds and stormy weather?

Consider: What is this step you want to take about? What is the value you want to serve? Why is it important for you to take the step while experiencing craving thoughts and feelings? Connect with your values and choose to take the step because it is important and has meaning for you to do so, even if difficult thoughts and emotions arise. Then choose to take another step in that direction, remembering you can always come to your "sky" perspective, your enduring self or the observer/noticer part of you.

Choice Moment Aids

You have gained additional aids in this chapter to help you on your valued-living path, as this figure shows. Continue to add the skills you use to your own Craving Choice Moment Diagram from the online free tools.

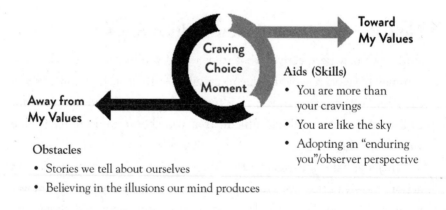

Toward My Values

Craving Choice Moment

Aids (Skills)
- You are more than your cravings
- You are like the sky
- Adopting an "enduring you"/observer perspective

Away from My Values

Obstacles
- Stories we tell about ourselves
- Believing in the illusions our mind produces

Bringing It All Together

- Our minds produce many *stories* about who we are and, by extension, what we are able to achieve in our life (such as stopping smoking, using, or overeating). These stories can be helpful sometimes, or they can get in the way of living the life we want and achieving the goals we want to achieve.

- These stories are not who we are. We are much more than the stories and all the internal events (thoughts, feelings, sensations, cravings) our mind produces. We are like the immense black sky. Our internal content is like the weather, the clouds, the stars, always changing; yet this content does not affect the sky, always present, there in the background.

- To connect with ourselves as being bigger than any of our internal experiences, we can link up to our *observer* self, which can observe or notice all these thoughts, feelings, cravings, and stories. Once we recognize that we are separate from the internal experiences and the stories, we can think or feel one way yet choose to act in a different, values-consistent way.

- Connecting with this observer, this enduring self, takes practice, noticing your internal experiences and also being aware that you are noticing them.

- Adopting an observer self perspective helps us with our behavioral choices and gives us the freedom and flexibility to head where we want our lives to go. It helps us overcome our cravings and change our addictive habits.

Bringing Our Learning to Life

The concepts we presented in this chapter are somewhat abstract and may be difficult to comprehend and connect with at first. We suggest that over the next few days you reread parts of this chapter and listen to the exercises.

We also suggest that you practice stepping back and noticing. Connect with the sky within you, and from that perspective notice and observe with curiosity all the "clouds" that show up. Explore the thoughts, feelings, sensations, cravings, stories. Notice how they change all the time. See if you can remain in the sky perspective and notice all internal experiences as just ever-changing clouds and stars in the sky.

Each day, choose one valued step or action, large or small, that you would like your self to take. Move slowly so you can notice each aspect of the step while remaining in contact with your observer self. Commit to taking this step while you take along for the ride all your "clouds," all your thoughts, feelings, and cravings.

In the next chapter, we will discuss how to use mindfulness as a skill to break free from being on "autopilot mode" in our daily lives.

CHAPTER 8

Mindfulness: Taming the Craving Horse

Alex   *I have spent the better part of my life lost in my thoughts. Either trying to relive the few good moments I had in life or dreading the bleak future. I drank and drank so that I would not think about all the horrible moments I experienced or the people I hurt or let down along the way. I drank so as not to remember all of the awful things I did and feel all the pain related to them. And while drinking, I would hurt myself and others more and I would have more things to regret and not want to remember. Thinking about the future hurt the most because I was afraid that my difficult experiences will continue. What future do I have? Some days I can't even see it. On other days, I feared about what the future will bring, because I was sure that it would be more of the same or worse. And I drank again and again. I am so tired of it all!*

As humans we have the capacity to use our minds to remember and recreate pasts long gone. We can think about all the mishaps we've had, all our embarrassing actions, and all our shortcomings. At any moment, a trigger may bring up any of these things, and what happens? We immediately feel similar emotions of embarrassment, shame, sadness, disappointment, pain, as if we were experiencing the same situation all over again. Then we may dive into thoughts of *Oh no, I would never want that to happen again!* This may take us to the future and raise worries about what it might bring. And all this can lead to cravings for the substance or food we are addicted to.

Being able to remember our past and think about the future serves a very important survival function. We learn from past experiences and prepare for potential problems. But what happens when we get stuck and cannot stop ruminating about the past or being overly worried about the future? The problem is not that we have this capability but that we get *stuck*—and stop living in the present.

EXERCISE: Thinking About the Past, Present, and Future

It can be helpful to draw circles in your notebook representing how much we think about the past, present, and future. The circle size represents how much time we think about each of them. Draw one circle to represent how much your mind drifts to things you have done in the past, both good times and any regrets. Now another circle for how much you think about the present, the here and now. Finally, draw a circle for how much you think about the future, including plans, worries, and work you need to get done. Now, what do those circles look like? If you are like most of us, their proportions are as shown in the figure.

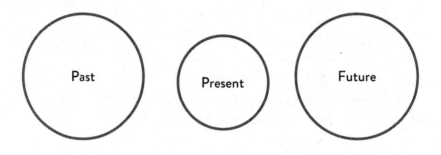

Many of us are living in our minds, thinking about the past and future, but not as much about the present. We get lost in our minds and lose our ability to function and respond in the here and now. We live in our heads, not in the present situation or environment. When this happens, we lose our ability to function based on our important values and where we want our lives to go. Instead, we get caught in the rip currents of thoughts, cravings, regrets, and fears.

Alex's story demonstrates all too well this struggle of getting caught up in the past and fears about the future.

Autopilot Mode

To demonstrate how we get lost in our thoughts and miss the present, consider times when you may have acted as if on autopilot. Have you ever gotten in your car to go somewhere and suddenly realized you were instead on your way to work or another regular destination? This happens to us (Maria and Megan) all the time. We mean to go to the grocery store, then find ourselves on the way to work, with no memory of how we got there. We hear this from others too. When we are on autopilot, a routine habit takes over. In this case, the action usually doesn't have big consequences; it just adds a little extra time to our day's chores. In other cases this may cause serious problems, as in the very tragic story of a doctor (his profession made it even more astounding) whose one-year-old son died from hyperthermia in his car. That morning the doctor had to take his son to day care, which was not part of his usual routine. The doctor drove to work, parked his car, and went about his busy workday on autopilot, forgetting the child in the car under the hot sun.

For individuals struggling with cravings, being on autopilot costs them their sobriety as they may mindlessly smoke a cigarette or have a drink and not even remember how either got in their hands. This also happens frequently with food. How many of us intend to take a handful of chips, but wind up mindlessly eating far more than that?

What are some things mindlessness and being on an autopilot have cost you? Write your answers down in your notebook.

Like Alex, you may have been going through much of your life mindlessly. Alex lives in his head, in the glorified or regretted past and the feared future, and while he spends time there, where is he not living? You guessed it! The present moment—in the here and now. So more moments and opportunities go by, and as soon as Alex realizes this, he regrets it and blames himself for being a loser. And when he feels this way, his cravings appear, and they are so hard to resist when going through life mindlessly.

Costs of Living on Autopilot

Research has examined the costs of living in an autopilot mode, and here are some of the main costs. See how these compare to the ones you wrote about in your notebook.

Cost #1: It Makes Us Unhappy and Leaves Us Unsatisfied

In a really cool study published in *Science* (Killingsworth & Gilbert, 2010), more than five thousand individuals were asked at unpredictable times during their day whether at that moment their mind was on task or wandering and how happy they were feeling. Interestingly, 47 percent of the time participants' minds were wandering, and those times were associated with feeling less happy. This correlates with what the individuals we work with tell us—that they feel unhappy, unsatisfied, and more worried and stressed when their minds take them to the past or future. This happens because when we focus internally on our past or future, we miss the chance to actually experience any good things that happen in the moment. We fail to savor the enjoyable moments. One client described this as trying to listen to his favorite music while wearing earplugs.

Cost #2: We Miss Out on the Present

Alex gave Maria a perfect example of this. He related that his daughter had come home excited about a good grade she got in science and started to tell him all about it. He was very happy about this event, and as he was listening to his daughter, his mind wandered to his past and how he used to be good in science and one of his teachers had told him that he should become an engineer. His mind then took him to some dark places: how he failed to go to college and make anything of himself. All this brought up the craving for a drink, and he stood up and said, "I need a drink." You can imagine the surprise and disappointment on his daughter's face. She got very upset and yelled, "Is that all you have to say to me? You need a drink? Why do I bother with you?" He immediately realized that his mind's wandering to the past had cost him the present. He'd been cut off from the reality in that moment and missed the chance to express his pride for his daughter's achievement, to connect with her, to demonstrate his true feelings for her. By losing ourselves in the past or the future, we miss out on what is happening or what we would like to do in the here and now.

Cost #3: Our Actions Are Not in the Direction of Our Values

Alex's experience demonstrates this cost all too well. Alex acted not based on his value of wanting to be a supportive and encouraging father. He did not express his pride to his daughter. He did not provide encouragement or support. Acting on autopilot, he mindlessly said that he needed a drink. This was definitely not the way he wanted to behave with his daughter.

When it comes to craving and addictive behaviors, when we are on autopilot and a craving shows up, we rush to satisfy it and reach for that craved food or substance. We ignore the reality that cravings are time-bound. They come and they go. On autopilot, we miss the initial signs of craving (maybe a physiological change, a specific feeling in the mouth) and a chance to act differently based on our values. The figure shows a typical craving wave. Individuals usually cannot stand it when the cravings get intense and end up eating, drinking, smoking, or using. When that happens, the craving drops. However, with the next craving they end up using again, pulled into the rip current of addictive behaviors. However, if we recognize the signs of cravings and understand their wave patterns and how they come and go in a few minutes, we can then ride the wave, choose our actions, and not give in to the craving with addictive behaviors.

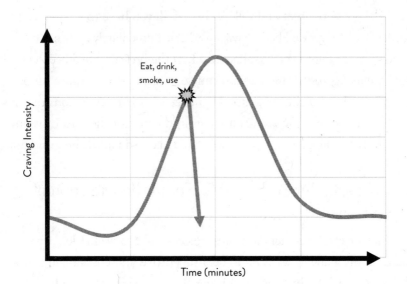

If Autopilot Costs So Much, Why Go There?

You may wonder: If going into a mindless mode is so bad, why do we do it? As with having thoughts and emotions, it serves several important purposes:

Autopilot Saves Time and Energy Do you remember when you learned how to tie your shoes, or the first time you sat in the driver's seat? You may recollect having to think about each step of the task, where each hand should go, what the next movement should be. It may have even seemed like an impossible endeavor to achieve. Yet with practice you mastered these tasks and they became automatic. Now when you tie your shoes or drive, you exert little mental energy to thinking about each step. You automated your actions to free up your thinking time and energy for other things. This is how habits for routine actions usually form, to serve the important function of helping save mental energy reserves for less familiar or repetitive matters that require concentration and mental effort.

Autopilot Helps Us Learn from Our Mistakes When our mind wanders to the past, and especially to mistakes we've made, we tend to go over the situation and consider what we did wrong or what we should have done differently. This is actually a good teaching practice. It can help us learn from past mistakes so we behave differently when faced with a similar situation in the future. Problems arise when we get stuck and ruminate over possible past mishaps, as we discussed in previous chapters.

Autopilot Helps Us Adapt to Be More Effective Thinking about the future and problems that may arise provides a very important survival advantage for us as humans. It prepares us for what may come and helps us find solutions for difficulties that may arise. This becomes problematic when we get stuck in the future, and especially when we lose ourselves in our fears and all that we dread may happen.

Autopilot Protects Us from Emotional Pain Losing ourselves in our thoughts serves an avoidance function, which, as we have seen, works well momentarily to relieve stress, fears, worries, and emotional pain. The key word is *momentarily*. It helps in the moment, but in the long run we have seen it create more problems, disconnection, and suffering.

Autopilot Provides Pleasure Reminiscing about any good old times or imagining things we want to do in the future, places we want to visit, or people we want to spend time with can provide pleasure and warm feelings. But even pleasurable feelings and thoughts can become triggers for craving. Again, this becomes counterproductive if we become stuck in dysfunctional thoughts of *I will never have this again,* or we choose to use, drink, or eat the craved substance.

Taming the Craving Horse

However helpful it is for our mind to go on autopilot, to visit the past or imagine the future, we know too well that it can lead us astray and down a craving path, which can take us back to using. But we can learn to tame our minds and our craving horse.

Do you have an image of how wild horses are tamed? You may be surprised to learn that nonforceful techniques are best, with the horse being let out on a very long rope and left in an open field. Feeling free, the horse runs around, and the trainer slowly draws in the rope until the horse gradually adapts and finally comes to a natural rest. The trainer then approaches, feeds, and pets the horse, and over time this process helps the trainer tame the horse.

We can take such a gentle approach with our minds. This is mindfulness. It involves *training ourselves to pay attention purposefully and flexibly, in the present moment and in a gentle, nonjudgmental way* (Kabat-Zinn, 2016). Let's unpack this definition and learn the tools of mindfulness.

The first part, *paying attention purposefully*, means bringing our attention, on purpose (getting out of autopilot mode), to something on either our inside (thoughts, feelings, memories) or our outside (an object, an activity, another human being, and so on). An easy practice of mindfulness entails bringing our attention to our breathing. We say it's easy because breathing is something we do without needing to think about it. Yet we can change our breathing at will—slow it down, speed it up, or make it deeper or shallower. We can also just pay attention and observe, which is the idea proposed in mindfulness. The next exercise involves this.

The next part of the definition refers to the *present moment* and suggests that we can pay attention only in the present. We cannot pay attention to something that happened hours, days, or years ago. We can only observe and explore what is happening in this moment.

The last part of the definition proposes that we *observe gently and without judgment.* Again, our minds are trained to judge, criticize, examine, compare, contrast, and so on. However, this takes us out of being in the present. But by gently and nonjudgmentally observing, we return from autopilot to the here and now. This is the only place from which we can actually act, problem solve, and make changes in our lives.

Embedded in the definition was also the concept of doing all of this *flexibly*. This suggests that if at times it is helpful to act on autopilot or wander off in our minds (say, mentally rehearse our plan for our daughter's surprise party), or problem solve (say, finding the best solution to a problem at work), then it is perfectly all right to do so and even helpful. So "flexibility" means differentiating when being in our heads or acting on autopilot is helpful and when it is not in accordance with our values and how we want to be behaving.

Let's give it a try. You've already practiced mindfulness in some of the previous chapters' exercises when you observed your thinking. Here, however, is a more classic mindfulness exercise. You can read the instructions here (better to read them a couple of times) and then practice it yourself—the exercise only takes a couple of minutes. You'll find recorded mindfulness exercises with the online free tools (http://www.newharbinger.com/48336).

EXERCISE: Mindfulness of the Breath

1. Find a place where you can sit or lie down comfortably. At least when you are learning the practice, choose a place that is quiet or at least where you won't be disturbed for the next few minutes.

2. Close your eyes or rest your gaze on a spot in the room.

3. Bring your attention with purpose to your breathing. Do not try to change it in any way. Just observe it as it is. Notice the air entering your nostrils, flowing into your body and down to your chest. Notice as the exhaled air comes out.

4. Pay attention to your breath in this moment. Notice the temperature of the air as it enters—maybe it is a bit cool—and then observe the air coming out, perhaps a bit warmer. Just notice how your chest rises with each inhale and falls with each exhale. Nothing too extreme. Just gently observing the breathing action.

5. When your mind wanders, notice where it has gone off to and gently bring it back. Remember, one aspect of mindfulness is paying attention nonjudgmentally, so if any judgment shows up, notice it and bring your attention back to the breath.

6. All you are doing is fully observing and engaging with your breathing. As if you have never before known what it is like to breathe. Appreciate how your body knows exactly how to do this activity that keeps you alive.

7. Continue for a couple of minutes or however long you feel like it. The exact amount of time you practice does not matter. What matters is that you pay attention, on purpose, in the here and now, and practice bringing back your wandering mind every time it goes on autopilot mode and travels to the past or the future. When sensations, feelings, or emotions show up, notice them, too, and bring your attention back to your breath.

How was this for you? What did you notice? Your mind probably wandered, because this is what our minds do. What's important is if your mind wanders a hundred times, you notice it and bring it back all hundred times. Did you bring your wandering mind back? Did you explore any judgments or comments your mind brought up about your experience or this exercise? There is no way to fail at this exercise. Whatever happened is all right.

Connecting to our breath has been described as dropping an anchor in the present moment (Harris, 2009). It is a way to ground ourselves on a stable base from which we can face the world and all that comes up in our lives, including cravings. Try this exercise daily and observe how each time new things appear. Over time it becomes easier to bring back your attention, and soon you will have tamed your craving horse.

Failing to Tame the Horse: Mindfulness Misconceptions

If you believe that you cannot do this, you are like most of us. You have had years of experience teaching your mind to go on autopilot and wander around. We assure you, it will not take so long to learn this new approach. However, it takes practice. Mindfulness is like a muscle: the more you practice, the stronger your skills will become and the easier it will get.

Some individuals reject the concept of mindfulness, based on misconceptions. Let us explore some of these:

I cannot stop thinking or *I cannot empty my head* or *I still get cravings.* Mindfulness is not about getting your mind to stop thinking, emptying your mind, or redirecting yourself away from cravings and difficult thoughts and emotions. We hope it's becoming clear that mindfulness is about observing and noticing whatever shows up. The aim is to recognize your thoughts and feelings as they unfold in the present. To notice the cravings when they show up. Once you notice, you will also notice that you are present and able to choose how you would like to respond to your thoughts and cravings.

I am not interested in getting pulled into religious or new-age practices. Individuals who express this fear tend to confuse mindfulness with meditative practices commonly associated with Eastern philosophies or religions or new-age culture. Though some of the exercises we use in mindfulness practices do resemble some forms of meditation, the aim here is not to connect with a higher power or to indoctrinate you in any sort of religious practice. We actually borrow from such religious practices those concepts that research has found are helpful and use them to fit our purpose—in this case, to bring our attention to the present moment and away from the labyrinth of our thoughts and emotions.

Further, we aim to provide you with the skills necessary to deal with your cravings and make changes in your life. You are free to choose those that are helpful for you and use those. Feel free to make them your own. Shortly we will give you more examples of how you can bring mindfulness into your life without doing any formal practice or closed-eye exercises, if you prefer.

I am trying these exercises, but I do not feel relaxed or able to think positively. For some individuals who engage in mindfulness exercises, relaxation or calmness may result as a side effect of paying attention, slowing down the mind's chatter, and observing. However, this is not the goal of mindfulness, nor is the goal to bring up "positive" thoughts and emotions. Quotes around the word "positive" signify that we believe that all emotions are just emotions, that they aren't inherently positive or negative. Delineating them as such is not particularly helpful.

When practicing mindfulness, it is actually common for difficult thoughts and emotions to show up. This provides great training opportunities for practicing the acceptance and defusion skills discussed in previous chapters. By observing thoughts and emotions, we start to see them in a different light, which may help us create space and bring about choice moments for engaging in valued actions.

More Ways to Become Mindful

There are additional ways to bring your attention to the here and now and connect you with your observer self; some examples follow. Be creative! Look for ways you can be mindful every day, from your routines (taking a shower, brushing your teeth, dressing and undressing, making the bed, driving to work, doing house chores, cooking) to your pleasurable activities or hobbies.

Notice with Your Five Senses

All humans have the ability to sense, though we don't all have function in all five senses: hearing, sight, smell, taste, and touch. Connecting to our senses is a great way to get grounded in the here and now. For example, if we asked you to feel the touch of the person you love the most on this planet, you would need to have them touch you this moment. You could of course describe this from memory, yet it is not the same as being touched this very moment. Similarly, if we asked you to taste your favorite food, you would be able to describe it from memory, yet to really taste it you would need to eat it at this moment and be connected to your sense of taste and smell. This goes for all the senses; whenever we notice our senses, we do so in the present moment; we can bring our attention to our senses and do it mindfully. So any time you find yourself lost in your thoughts, drawn into the past or the future, struggling with your cravings, you can bring your awareness to your senses as follows:

Notice three things using your senses. Here are some examples and a chance for you to practice noticing using your senses. Note things you notice in your notebook.

Sight: I can see a painting of a flower hanging on the wall, I see my blue notebook on my desk, I see [fill in, in your notebook].

Hearing: I hear my son playing the guitar, I hear a car honking outside, I hear [fill in].

Touch: I feel my feet touching the floor, I feel my hands touching the computer keyboard, I feel [fill in].

Smell: I smell lemon flowers on the lemon tree outside my window, I smell [fill in].

Taste: I taste the sweet, sour, and somewhat bitter taste of fresh lemonade, I taste [fill in].

When you notice your surroundings using your senses, you will be in the present. Soon enough, your mind will wander again and pull you away. That is fine. As soon as you notice that's happened, come back to your senses and the present.

What did you manage to notice using your senses? How was this for you? Did your mind bring up any judgments or criticize you? Could you notice that and return to your senses (literally and metaphorically)? Can you bring this mindfulness attention to your values as well?

Notice Your Thoughts

We actually have already practiced a similar exercise, the Leaves on a Stream exercise. Feel free to go back and repeat that exercise. The idea with noticing your thoughts is to bring curiosity to your observation and to look at each thought nonjudgmentally from an observer perspective. Here is another exercise (you'll find an audio version with the online free tools):

EXERCISE: Mindfulness of Thoughts and Cravings
(based on Harris, 2019)

1. Find a place where you can sit or lie down comfortably. At least when you are learning the practice, choose a place that is quiet or where you won't be disturbed for the next few minutes.

2. Close your eyes or rest your gaze on a spot in the room.

3. Bring your attention to your thoughts, especially on thoughts related to cravings. With curiosity, explore: Where are your thoughts? What are your thoughts like? Are they like a voice? Where is the voice located? Is it inside your head? Near your ears?

4. Notice the form of your thoughts. Are they like pictures, or are they more like words?

5. Are the thoughts moving or still? If they are moving, how fast or slow do they move? If they are still, where are they resting?

6. Notice the environment around the thoughts. How do the thoughts relate to each other? Are they touching or are they on top of each other? Are there spaces in between them?

7. For a couple of minutes now, watch your thoughts coming and going. Watch with curiosity, as if you have never seen such thoughts before. If you get stuck with any thought, just let it hang out; do not try to push it away or force it in any way.

8. Acknowledge any difficult thoughts or cravings: *Here is this old craving again.* Notice these cravings for what they are—just words. Just observe them without any attempt to change them, push them away, or hold on to them. Just let them be there, and watch them as you would watch an interesting documentary on a screen.

9. If you do get pulled in by these thoughts and lose track of what you are doing, know that this is absolutely normal. As soon as you notice this, gently acknowledge it and return to observing the thoughts again.

10. Now slowly bring your attention back to the room. Notice where you are, and when you are ready, open your eyes. Look around you and notice what you see and hear. Welcome back!

Engage In and Be Present for Pleasurable Activities

In the next exercise, you'll think of a pleasurable activity—not one involving your addictive behavior, but one you tend to do on autopilot. Examples: drinking a glass of cold water, savoring your favorite flavor of tea, eating a juicy orange, dancing, playing an instrument, listening to music, watering plants, exercising, playing with a pet—the list goes on. We present one example to get you started; make it your own. Maria loves to paint, so she used this example to demonstrate how you can paint mindfully.

EXERCISE: Mindfully Painting (or Other Favorite Activity)

Bring your attention to your chosen activity. Connect with what is important—perhaps it's the value this activity serves for you. For me, painting connects me with my value of creating, expressing, learning, and appreciating.

Throughout this exercise, different thoughts and feelings will show up. Let them come and go, and keep your attention on the exercise. If you realize that your attention has wandered, briefly note what distracted you, then bring your attention back to the activity.

Engage with your painting using your senses. What do you see? Look at the lines, shapes, forms, textures, and colors created. Notice how the light hits the canvas or paper and the paints. What do you smell? Depending on the medium you use, there may be distinct paint smells you are able to explore.

What do you feel? How does it feel to be holding the brush, to gently push the brush into the paint and mix the colors up? How does it feel to move the brush across a surface? Imagine that this is the first time you ever engaged in the activity; bring in all the curiosity you would have as a novice. Like a child being given brushes and paints for the first time, explore every aspect from this fresh perspective.

What do you hear when the brush is mixing the paints? What do you hear when the brush moves over the paper or canvas? Listen carefully to even the small sounds.

How does your body move while you paint? How are your hands moving?

Again, notice any thoughts or feelings when they show up. Watch them come and go, and intentionally bring your attention back to painting and appreciate this time you are spending with this medium and connecting with your values.

How was each of these exercises for you? What sort of thoughts showed up? What was it like to observe your thoughts and craving and letting them just be there? Did you find yourself trying to push certain thoughts away? Were there others you tried hard to hold on to? All of these responses are normal; the important thing is that you noticed all this happening and returned to observing and paying attention either to your breath, your body, or the task you were engaging in.

Mindfulness Takes Practice

We can bring focus and attention to anything we do in our daily lives, so there are literally hundreds of ways we can be more mindful and hundreds of opportunities for us to practice this skill. We provided examples for ways you can practice, and we invite you to find your own examples. There are many apps for mindfulness exercises. The more you practice bringing attention and purpose to what you do, the more benefits you will see from the practice. These include saving time—you will not, for example, drive elsewhere when you wanted to go to the grocery store, or need to return home to check whether you unplugged the iron. You will save your energy, become more connected with your loved ones, and enhance the pleasure you get from activities. Even when we're engaged in not-so-pleasurable activities, paying attention helps us notice there may actually be some parts that are not so bad. With regard to cravings, you will be able to make room for them and choose how you want to act, whether they show up or not; you will no longer be their prisoner. And cravings may even decrease over time.

Choice Moment Aids

In this chapter we recognized how being on autopilot may act as an obstacle to values-based living and an "away" action. We learned the skill of mindfulness as an antidote to being on autopilot and learned various ways we can act mindfully in our daily lives. This figure depicts this choice moment. You can use the Craving Choice Moment Diagram with the online free tools to list all your aids and skills.

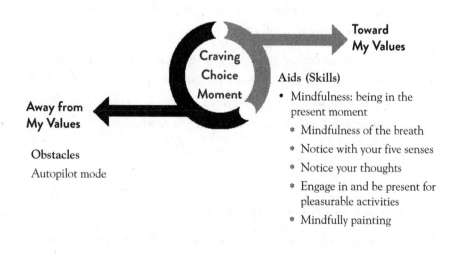

Toward
My Values

Craving
Choice
Moment

Aids (Skills)
• Mindfulness: being in the present moment
   * Mindfulness of the breath
   * Notice with your five senses
   * Notice your thoughts
   * Engage in and be present for pleasurable activities
   * Mindfully painting

Away from
My Values

Obstacles
Autopilot mode

Bringing It All Together

- In our daily life we are used to being enthralled with our thoughts; we live in the past or the future and miss living in the here and now.

- We do this so much that we mindlessly get in an autopilot mode of functioning. Thus we miss out on important life moments, get cut off from interacting with loved ones, and end up doing things that are not aligned with our values or what we care about. We may enhance thoughts and feelings of craving, putting ourselves at risk for getting into addictive behaviors.

- Of course, the autopilot mode serves us well in many areas in our lives, so we get caught up in it and don't really notice it.

- Mindfulness—the skill of training ourselves to pay attention purposefully and flexibly, in the present, gently and nonjudgmentally —is the antidote to all this.

- Mindfulness takes practice. Fortunately, there are hundreds of ways to be mindful in everyday life—simply use your breath to anchor you to the present and your senses and curiosity to observe either something in your surroundings or what goes through your mind or body.

Bringing Our Learning to Life

Because mindfulness takes practice, we invite you to take all that we've discussed in this chapter and bring it to your life. Try to practice a mindfulness exercise once a day and see how you benefit. You can practice mindfulness anytime and anywhere. You can do any activity mindfully by connecting with the present moment and observing using your senses, noticing all the internal stuff that shows up, nonjudgmentally and with curiosity.

Sometimes our clients tell us that they meant to practice, yet things got in the way. Observing what got in the way (internal or external) can also be part of mindfulness practice. So if you notice things getting in the way of you doing anything you find important or practicing any of the skills you learned in this book, you will be practicing mindfulness.

In the next chapter, we will discuss how self-stigma interferes with values-based living, and we'll introduce self-compassion as the antidote.

CHAPTER 9

Making Friends with Ourselves: Self-Compassion as the Antidote to Self-Stigma

Alex   *I tried many times to cut back on drinking, yet I am weak, and I guess I lack willpower to be able to achieve it. I know I am a loser; I always let others down, and most of all I let myself down. That is how "drunks" are—losers through and through! I thought that if I got a job, it would take my mind off drinking and I could get my life together. But who would want to hire a drunk? Who wants to work with a loser?*

Amy   *I am weak! If I were strong, I would be able to withstand the craving and not give in. Is there a point in even trying? I do not think I can ever stop. I have thought of reaching out for help so many times, but I am not sure it will help at all. I feel really sad and hopeless about my situation. Of course, all this brings up more cravings, and I just want to eat my comfort food. And then I feel disgusted at myself. What sort of a role model am I for my kids? I embarrass myself and them at every turn.*

Self-Defeating Cycles of Stigma and Shame

In Alex's and Amy's statements you may have recognized some beliefs that they hold about themselves that mainly embody how others regard individuals with addictive problems. Shame and stigma are evident in their words. Research on stigma in relation to addictive behaviors is still in its infancy, yet it is recognized more and more as a crucial issue that hinders recovery. Interestingly, stigma shows up not just from others toward the person suffering from an addictive problem, but also from the person themself. This is called *self-stigma*. We discussed self-stigma already when we talked about the stories we buy into about ourselves (see chapter 7). We also recognized self-stigma's sibling, shame. Shame involves evaluating oneself negatively or perceiving oneself as flawed.

Self-stigma and shame are negative thoughts we have about ourselves. When a person becomes fused with these thoughts, the person falls into a self-defeating cycle and fails to see their specific behaviors in a situation. For example, Alex blamed his not getting hired on being unreliable and a loser, rather than focusing on how he presented and behaved during the job interview. By emphasizing the behavior here, we are not *blaming* the person; however, we are trying to demonstrate that he is *responsible* in that he is *able to make a response*. Recognizing that we can choose the response and behavior we want is an extremely important part of dealing with self-stigma and shame. As we've said throughout this book, we want to turn our energy and focus toward changing the things we can (our behavior) rather than continue to struggle with the things we cannot change (sticky thoughts that our mind produces).

This figure depicts Alex's self-defeating cycle.

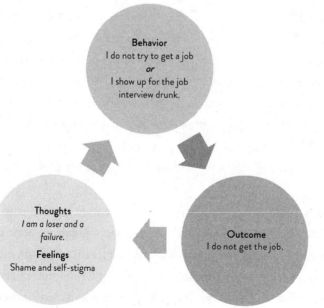

Behavior
I do not try to get a job
or
I show up for the job
interview drunk.

Outcome
I do not get the job.

Thoughts
*I am a loser and a
failure.*
Feelings
Shame and self-stigma

EXERCISE: Acknowledging Stereotypes

Let's examine the types of stereotypes or biases we have. Notice the impression you formed about Alex based on the information we provided in the previous chapter and in this chapter. What do you think about Alex? Write down in your notebook a few of the ways you would characterize him.

Some people, reading the descriptions here, would characterize him as someone with a problem with alcohol, which makes him irresponsible, a loser who has done hurtful or harmful things to himself or others and most likely has let down others.

Let us now give you some more information about Alex. Alex grew up in a very difficult environment. His father had an alcohol problem; he would often drink and hit Alex, his mother, and his younger sister. When Alex was thirteen, his father once came home drunk and started beating up his younger sister. Alex's mother, desperate to save her daughter, took a kitchen knife and stabbed his father. His father died, and his mother was incarcerated. Alex and his sister went into foster care. Alex felt a strong need to protect his younger sister. At seventeen, Alex returned to the foster home he and his sister were staying at for a few months and found the foster dad molesting his sister (then twelve years old). He reacted by grabbing a knife and stabbing the foster dad. Though the foster dad did not die, Alex was sent to prison for five years. It preyed on him that he did not protect his sister and that he abandoned her. He started drinking in prison, as that was the only thing that would take the pain away.

How would you characterize Alex now that you know more about his story? Write your response in your notebook.

How does your perception of Alex differ now from what you first wrote? Your perceptions or judgment of Alex may have changed as you learned more about his struggles in life. You may even excuse Alex's behavior, and if now you had him in front of you, you would want to comfort him or show compassion.

This demonstrates our human tendency to judge, evaluate, or categorize individuals based on limited information—judging a book by its cover. Though this can serve us well (such as being efficient at processing information) and make functioning more efficient (like autopilot mode—we get to things faster this way), it can lead to snap judgments, whereby we use limited information or certain characteristics to judge others and pigeon-hole them as stereotypes. Interestingly, we extend these stereotypes to ourselves as well; we then judge and criticize ourselves, falling into a self-defeating cycle. We may even fool ourselves that these judgments serve to get us motivated to change. Let's put this to the test.

EXERCISE: The Judgment Bully

Imagine you are trying to do a task—cooking, house chores, gardening, learning a new skill or a new language, anything that comes to mind. Now imagine that you have the meanest teacher or coach ever standing next to you, yelling directions and comments. This is the worst bully you have ever met, screaming at you: "You are stupid! You are a loser! You cannot do this. You are a [insert here any of the labels you tend to give yourself]. You amount to nothing. There is no way you're going to do this right." Write in your notebook what this bully tells you.

How do you feel? Do you feel motivated to do the task? Would you want your child to have this person as a teacher or coach? If you are like most of us, you will probably feel demotivated and want to give up. Research supports this, suggesting that the more critical we are of ourselves, the less motivated we are to change, the more cravings we have, and the more we engage in self-defeating behaviors like overeating, smoking, drinking, or using drugs.

Take a few moments now and engage your observer self to recognize the self-defeating cycles you put yourself in. With the online free tools you will find a My Self-Defeating Cycles diagram that you can use.

We've seen that there is no way to stop our minds from producing self-critical thoughts and feelings. But recognizing these cycles and using the skills we've learned so far can help set us free from these self-defeating cycles. Skills of cognitive defusion, observer self, recognizing what is of most value to us, and connecting with the present moment have already headed us in the direction in which we want to go. In this chapter, we will learn an additional skill that will help us achieve a different perspective, which will be the antidote to our criticizing self. This skill is called self-compassion.

Self-Compassion: The Antidote to Self-Defeating Cycles

We have already touched on how to develop self-compassion. If you have started to recognize yourself as separate from the stories your mind produces, envisioning yourself as being like the vast black sky, and connecting with your observer self, then you are already becoming more self-compassionate. One aspect of self-compassion is mindfulness—observing, noticing, and being present nonjudgmentally (Neff, 2003). As you start to pay attention and connect with the here and now, you are on your way to becoming more self-compassionate. Another important part of self-compassion is starting to recognize that you are human—and humans make mistakes, have setbacks and insecurities, fall into self-defeating behaviors, feel disappointment and inadequacy, and have recurring thoughts and emotions that they struggle with. Realizing that all these are part of a shared human experience, and that suffering is not just a personal and isolated event, opens us up to our *common humanity*.

Another aspect of self-compassion concerns self-kindness: being caring, loving, and compassionate toward oneself. Remember the critical bully teacher/coach example, and how you feel when this person shouts all those mean things at you.

Now let's try it differently.

EXERCISE: The Compassionate Teacher or Coach

Imagine a kind, loving, caring, and compassionate teacher or coach. In a soft, warm voice, they tell you: *I know this is not easy. I believe in you. It takes practice, and you will get there. You have skills, and I know you can apply them. Even if you fail along the way, I am here to help you get back up. You can do it!*

Write in your notebook how this makes you feel. Would you want your child to have this person as a teacher? Note whether this voice makes you more motivated to do the task. You will probably recognize that you are more motivated and more likely to try harder when you hear these words over the words of the mean bully. When we have such encouragement, even when we fail, we are more likely to get up and try again.

Now read the following questions and write your answers in your notebook.

- What kind of a teacher/coach are you for yourself?

- Consider the things that you tend to say to yourself. Would you say those things to another person, especially one who has had life throw all kinds of difficulties at them and is trying to get back on their feet? Would you say these things to a friend, a loved one, a child?

- If you said such things to them, how would they react? Would they want to be your friend, your confidant?

- Why would you want an unsympathetic critic to be your friend, your supporter? Wouldn't you prefer a compassionate teacher or coach instead?

Talking to yourself in such a kind, compassionate manner is an important skill for overcoming cravings. Before we further explore this self-compassion skill, let's discuss some pitfalls that may show up to sabotage your efforts to learn and practice this skill.

Self-Compassion Pitfalls

When we bring up the term *self-compassion* or the concept of bringing kindness to oneself even when experiencing cravings and other intense thoughts and emotions, some individuals react with skepticism. The word "self-compassion" may bring up eye-rolling associations: it's touchy-feely, new-agey, or even religious. Notice that these are judgments produced by our mind and relate to things we may have heard or learned from our culture. If you have this reaction, simply acknowledge it and read on to hear more about the self-compassion story. Your perspective of this concept may change, as you recognize that all humans need self-compassion and that practicing it will actually strengthen you to handle life with all its difficulties and problems. Alex, for example, initially thought self-compassion was a new-age type of concept. But learning about self-care, kindness, and compassion helped him see its value. By the end of therapy, he said it was one of his favorite and most helpful skills that he gained in therapy.

Some of our clients have been confused about self-compassion; they believed that by smoking, drinking, eating excessively, or using substances, they were offering themselves kindness and pleasure. Amy, for example, said her "comfort food," especially sweets, gave her soothing, warm feelings. This, however, is a mind trap, an illusion. You have come to associate these behaviors with pleasure—at times they have seemed to be your only friends. But consider whether these are truly kind to your body, your health, your well-being, your loved ones. Are these the kinds of friends you want? Do they really help you overcome your cravings, or do they contribute to making them worse in the long run? Do they help you get on your valued path in life? We hope that by now you recognize that they do no such things; rather, they move you away from your values with the illusion of support, pleasure, and temporary relief from cravings. A kind, compassionate friend would not harm your body, your health, your mind, or your functionality, or trick you into becoming addicted, or exacerbate your cravings.

What kind of a helper, advocate, friend do you want? Probably one who offers support, especially when things are hard; who cares about what you value and offers wise advice to help you with your cravings and the actions you want to take in life.

Enhancing Life with Self-Compassion

An effective way to enhance your life with self-compassion is to start treating yourself with kindness and care, especially when you suffer, face cravings, or fall back into a self-defeating cycle. Here's a simple formula: (1) acknowledge the suffering, the difficulty, the mistake you made, and (2) purposefully respond to yourself with acceptance and kindness, reminding yourself of the choices you have in this moment. Use words like *This hurts/ feels bad, and I will go easy with myself, be gentle and kind*, or *This is disappointing and shows that I am human and I can choose how to act differently in this moment*. Find your own words to help you acknowledge the difficulty and extend self-compassion to yourself. Write your words in your notebook.

There are many ways you can practice self-compassion: listening to your favorite music; visiting a gallery or a museum to enjoy gazing around at beautiful creations; going to a park to sit, watch, and appreciate the nature around you; going to the beach and walking barefoot on the sand or collecting seashells. Make your own list. Brainstorm some things you enjoy doing—satisfying pleasures that don't relate to your cravings or addictive behaviors. Write your list in your notebook.

While you engage in each of these activities, remind yourself that this is a special activity that you chose to engage in and that you deserve to enjoy. Remind yourself this is something you would recommend to a friend, and that you deserve the same compassion and loving-kindness you would extend to others.

Similarly, when a craving shows up, it is a good chance for us to practice our self-compassion. The following is a guided mindfulness exercise; you can record your own version or download an audio file from the online free tools at http://www.newharbinger.com/48336.

EXERCISE: Craving Kindness

Start by taking a few deep, slow breaths, noticing how your abdomen rises with each inhalation, then falls with each exhalation. Rest the tip of your tongue gently against the roof of your mouth, just behind your upper front teeth. Smile gently, noticing your lips as they spread out and lift just slightly—a kind smile, like the one in Da Vinci's *Mona Lisa*, or how you might smile—mostly to yourself—if you've just gotten a joke that someone told you several days ago. Nothing extreme...

Now bring your attention to the space between your eyebrows. As you rest your attention there, energy may begin to gather. Imagine it as a pool of warm water. Let your attention slowly dive deeper into that pool...back and toward the center of your brain. Let your attention rest there for a few moments. This is a really powerful place in your brain, home to important glands involved in the experience of emotions. Send some smiling energy to that part of your brain and let the energy gather up and pool there...

Slowly allow this energy to flow forward into your eyes. Let your eyes become "smiling eyes." Imagine that you are gazing into the eyes of the person you love the most in this world...and they are gazing back at you...infusing your eyes with this quality of loving-kindness and delight.

Now take a few moments to visit with your craving. Consider how it is affecting you or how it usually makes you act. Notice any associated thoughts, feelings, and sensations that arise. Notice them with curiosity, with a fresh perspective, as if you have never experienced such a craving, emotions, thoughts, or sensations before. Where do you feel this craving, the thoughts, the sensations in your body? Are they in your head, your mouth, your stomach, your hands? Notice them as if you are an explorer discovering new and mesmerizing lands. What are this craving, the thoughts, the sensations like? What shape, color, size are they? What is their temperature? Explore them with curiosity...

Now direct the energy of your smiling eyes to this craving and its associated thoughts and feelings, or the place where you usually may feel this craving within you. Smile down into that place in your body, and feel that place opening to receive your smiling energy. Continue to smile into that place in your body for as long as you like. Let the loving-kindness flow from your eyes and your mouth all the way to each spot that needs this kind energy, letting it soak up smiling energy as a sponge soaks up water. See if you can infuse this part of you with compassion, care, and support. If you notice a buildup of tension anywhere, visit that place and extend some of that same smiling energy to it as well. If your mind wanders, simply notice this, and come back to your gentle smile, to noticing, to extending loving-kindness and compassion to yourself.

Rest in this place and take a moment to consider how all that you are struggling with is an integral part of being human. Recognize that all humans struggle with something, whether it is cravings, thoughts, or feelings. You are not alone in this. You are only a human who hurts where you care. This is part of who you are, of being human.

When this feels complete, direct your inner gaze, with its smiling energy, to your navel center, feeling warmth and brightness gathering in your lower belly. Release the tip of your tongue from the roof of your mouth, and release the smile (or keep it, if it now feels natural). Notice the messages you send to your body, your mind, and to the world when you smile. Know that any time you need some smiling energy, you can give it to yourself. You can allow yourself to be who you are—perfectly imperfect, unique, whole, and vulnerable like everyone else.

This exercise has its roots in the Taoist tradition and specifically, the "inner smile meditation." To Maria this is one of the most powerful exercises and one she often uses herself when struggling with difficulties. She also uses it with almost all her clients because of its power to help the person better connect with themselves and provide the self-kindness and compassion that has been greatly lacking in their life. We usually ask clients to consider whether they'd want to have a friend who would talk to them as they normally talk to themselves. The answer is usually no. By practicing self-compassion and self-kindness, you will make friends with yourself and stop being your own worst enemy. That can lead to change and life enhancement.

The next exercise involves writing a love letter to yourself (adapted from Lillis, Dahl, & Weineland, 2014).

EXERCISE: Writing a Love Letter to Yourself

In your notebook, write a letter from your present perspective, addressed to yourself at some point in the past. Choose a time when you experienced something that shook you up or created shame and regret, or when you gave in to cravings and addictive behaviors. Whatever you prefer is fine. No one will read this letter if you do not want to share it.

Follow these steps:

1. Start by addressing the letter to yourself: "Dear..."

2. Briefly describe the situation, making sure to include your feelings and thoughts at the time.

3. Add the actions you chose to take at that time.

4. Next, consider what you would say to a dear friend or a loved one if they described going through such a situation themselves. How would you express your love and compassion for them? Write how you understand their pain, shame, anxiety, fears, and other emotions. Write that you support, forgive, and love them no matter what the situation was. Now write these things to your past self. Extend love, kindness, gratitude, compassion.

5. Close by redirecting yourself to your chosen values path and how you would like to act now.

This may feel awkward. If it does for you, recognize this and give it a try anyway. This is new; you have probably never talked to yourself in this way. It takes practice to change how you relate to yourself and to become more self-compassionate. To help you, here is the letter Alex wrote to his past self.

Dear Alex,

You were only seventeen when you did a terrible thing. Your anger blinded you, and you pulled a knife and stabbed that man. You were blinded by the fear and anger you felt. This landed you in jail for five years. You panicked when you heard this. You did not want to desert your sister. You left her helpless and alone. The regret was overwhelming you. Only the bottle could provide some numbness, stop you from feeling the worry, the fear, the disappointment. And you chose to drink at every opportunity. You were just a kid. Just a kid! A kid who was handed a shitty life. You had every right to feel scared. You tried to protect your sister. You tried to do the best you could. You did not want to see her get hurt. I understand that when you landed in the can you had no skills to help you manage all the emotions that were drowning you. I forgive you for what you did. I love you, and I will support you as you deal with all the things life throws at you. I appreciate how you are trying to rise above it all, and I want to see you succeed and rebuild your relationships. I am here for you, always.

Now it is your turn. As you write your love letter, be honest and genuine. Make sure to follow the exercise steps, including all components.

What did you notice as you were writing the letter? Perhaps your mind was pushing and pulling, bringing up thoughts that you do not deserve forgiveness, compassion, or love. Recognize that these are your thoughts and remember how we tame the wild horse when it pulls and resists—we give it some space and slowly rein it in. Practice all the skills we learned in this book, and come back to doing what matters to you. Offer compassion and support to yourself, however uncomfortable it might feel. When you're finished, put the letter away for a day or so. Then reread it, absorbing the message you are conveying—that no matter what you did in the past, you are worthy of kindness and love, and today you can choose a new path for your life.

Some individuals struggle with self-compassion exercises at the beginning, especially if they have had a long history of being harsh with themselves. Yet with practice, they get easier and produce fruitful results. We invite you to practice this and other self-compassion exercises and examine what changes might happen for you and how you deal with cravings. For example, Amy had such a long history of speaking harshly to herself, and of hearing others label her with similar unkind adjectives, that at first she had a lot of resistance to this concept of self-compassion. It felt really foreign to her, and she thought it would make her even weaker when facing her cravings. Yet slowly and with practice, she started to change. She was able to observe when cravings showed up and how this immediately triggered her negative, critical self-talk. At that point she acknowledged how important it was for her to talk to herself, and she began to offer herself love, kindness, compassion, and forgiveness. She was able to break free from the self-defeating cycles and enter into a self-enhancing mode. In one session she expressed that she could not believe the difference practicing self-compassion has made to her life, her cravings, and her eating behavior.

This figure depicts Amy's new self-enhancing mode of functioning in a choice moment:

Toward My Values

Life-Enhancing Behavior
- Use my therapy skills.
  * Remember my valued path.
  * Practice acceptance, cognitive defusion, mindfulness, self-compassion.

Away from My Values

Self-Defeating Behavior
- Eat comfort food
- Overeat

Craving Triggers, Associated Thoughts
- Is there a point in even trying?
- I don't think I can ever stop.

Feelings
- I feel weak.
- I feel a strong desire and my heart beating.

Choice Moment Aids

Use the blank diagram with the online free tools to expand your charting of your own self-enhancing mode of functioning. We suggest that you make it specific to the self-enhancing behaviors you would like to do. List the aids you like the best or help you the most, so you have them available when you need them. We suggest printing this diagram out and posting it at home where you can easily see it and remind yourself, when the craving shows up, how you would like to behave and what you choose to do.

Bringing It All Together

- We all fall into self-defeating cycles of shame and dwell on things we may regret having done in the past, blaming ourselves for failures to manage our cravings and change our addictive behaviors. Recognizing these self-defeating cycles is a major first step in making changes today.

- Self-compassion—the skill of acknowledging that you are human, just like everyone else, of returning to the present, and of choosing to act with kindness, gratitude, compassion, and love toward yourself—is the antidote to your self-defeating cycles. It offers a place of stability and strength from which you can choose how you want to act toward yourself and others.

- Self-compassion takes practice. We offered a number of ways to practice it, such as choosing to behave in ways that matter to you, doing activities that give you meaning and move you in the direction of living in accordance with your values, a craving kindness mindfulness exercise, and writing a love letter to yourself.

- Using self-compassion is another skill you can add to the toolbox you've been building up throughout this book, which can help you move toward a self-enhancing mode of functioning.

Bringing Our Learning to Life

As with the other skills learned in this book, incorporating these skills and practicing them in your life is the critical next step. We encourage you to embrace self-compassion in your life and practice little acts of compassion, kindness, and gratitude toward yourself throughout your days. Connect with your choices and behave in ways that matter to you, then recognize and acknowledge your efforts. Do things that you find worthwhile, engage in activities that stimulate and give you vitality, connect with others and foster caring for yourself physically and emotionally. We recommend keeping a self-compassion journal, in which you write at least one act you do each day for yourself that provides gratitude, care, love, support, and kindness and gives you vitality. Do this in conjunction with your values-driven actions.

In the next chapter, we will help you refocus on what is important to you and take actionable steps to improving your life.

CHAPTER 10

Having Your Cravings
and Living Too

Amy *I have tried several new techniques—mindfulness and acceptance—
and I am coping much better with my cravings. But giving up sweets has me
feeling like I am missing something. I used to look forward to rewarding myself
with sweets at the end of a hard day and eating them when I was stressed out.
Now that I don't eat sweets during those times, I feel like I am missing something. Also, since I am more aware of my values, I realize that there are a lot of
goals I want to accomplish for myself. I am trying to figure out my next steps.*

Revisiting Your Values

In chapter 3, we looked at our values and hopefully discovered what gives
our life meaning. These values are critical directions—lighthouses in the
storm. They can also provide guidance for changing our lives in new,
meaningful, and helpful ways. Now that we've been working on imple-
menting new skills in managing our cravings and addictive behaviors, let's
assess where this has led us.

Imagine that you are one hundred years old, and family and friends are
gathered to celebrate this momentous birthday. You overhear a conversation in the next room between your loved ones. They are talking about you
and your life. What would you like to hear them say? Toward the end of
your life, what would you most want people to be discussing about you?
What would you want them to be celebrating? What would family members
say? What would friends say? Think about what you would like to hear
them speak of, not what you think they will actually say. Say what you

would like, not whether you think it is unattainable or true at this point in time. This is what you would like your life to stand for.

It's time to revisit the Values Exercise that you completed in chapter 3 and fill out a fresh version. Has anything changed for you since you completed it earlier? Has your perception of what's important to you changed at all, or is it pretty much the same? Is the gap between the values that are important to you and how you are actually living any smaller now? If now there is no gap, that means that you are making progress. If there is a gap, let's do a little more work to help you make that gap even smaller or bridge it completely.

Living a Values-Based Life

We often feel deprived when we give up some type of addictive behavior. And then we may be in danger of filling that gap with another type of addictive behavior. If you give up drinking, you may end up smoking more. If you give up smoking, you might fill that gap with eating more.

But it doesn't have to be this way. There is another option: to fill your life with activities that directly align with your values. Whenever you take something out of your life, it leaves a hole that you want to fill. But it's your choice to fill that void with either healthy or unhealthy things. It's your chance to fill that void with activities that are in line with your values or those that get you closer to where you want to be. We call this *committed action*. This will also help close that gap between your values and how you've been living up to them. The smaller that gap, the more rewarding you will find your life becoming.

Now let's talk about how you put committed action into practice. (If you've practiced any of the techniques or skills we talked about throughout this book, you've already engaged in committed action.) Pick one or two of your highest-rated values—particularly the values where the gap between how important they are and how much you are living up to them is a little wider than with the rest. Think about some activities that you might be able to pursue that will help you close that gap. We provided a list of activities to get you started brainstorming and finding some that would be meaningful for you. Please consider your own ideas—activities that will bring you rewards, vitality, and joy. Committed action involves both physical actions (what you do with your body, your voice) or psychological action (mindfulness, cognitive defusion from thoughts, self-compassion).

Ideas for Committed Action Activities

- Listening to music (audiotape, CD, MP3, and so on)
- Going to parties or receptions
- Organizing a social gathering
- Playing board games with friends or family
- Mindfulness exercises
- Watching an interesting documentary
- Planning a vacation
- Reading
- Going to the library
- Charity work or volunteering
- Welcoming a new neighbor
- Joining a choral singing group
- Playing a musical instrument
- Meditating
- Doing yoga
- Drawing or painting
- Doing craft work (woodworking, pottery, quilting)
- Photography and filming
- Going fishing
- Gardening, taking care of plants
- Taking care of a pet

- Visiting friends or family

- Having a meal with friends or family

- Having a conversation with a neighbor

- Having coffee or tea with friends, family, and others

- Writing an email to friends, family, or colleagues

- Calling friends or family

- Having an online call with friends or family

- Meeting someone new

- Birdwatching

- Starting or joining a community garden

- Asking for help or advice

- Offering to help someone in need

- Giving someone a hug

- Going out on a date

- Giving someone a compliment

- Telling a loved one that you care for them

- Getting a medical checkup

- Improving your health (losing weight, changing what you eat, exercising)

- Engaging in self-compassionate talk and exercises

- Cooking or baking

- Participating in a sports league

- Helping coach youth sports

- Writing

- Hiking, camping, exploring, and other activities in nature

- Giving to a local food bank

- Starting a group chat with your extended family

- Joining your local community's group on Facebook or Nextdoor

- Starting or joining a book or film club

- Getting involved in community theater

- Volunteering to help your local senior centers, home care facilities, hospitals

- Engaging in an online course, from a program like Coursera

- Joining a cooking class

- Finding an exercise class

- Playing games with friends or family or using apps like Words with Friends or Jackbox

- Calling an old friend

- Other: _____

It is important to actually schedule these activities! These committed action activities will help to fill that void you might feel when you stop participating in addictive behaviors, and they will also feel more satisfying, because they are goals in line with your values.

Here are some guidelines to help you choose goals that will fill up your life with values-consistent activities.

- Choose one valued life domain that your goal will be in the service of, such as health, relationships, friendship, family, work. Link specific values to the domain you chose (for example, being loving toward my spouse, being more caring toward my friend).

- Choose a goal motivated by your values in step 1.

- Be specific and detailed; instead of "talking to friends" or "spending more time with family," make an actual schedule: "From 4 to 6 p.m. on Thursday, meet with Linda to go shopping at the mall."

- Goals should be easy to accomplish. Particularly if they are an activity that will fill the void when you've stopped unhealthy eating, drinking, using drugs, or smoking, you will want to find activities you can enjoy that are inexpensive, can be done frequently, and are rewarding.

- Smaller steps are often better than bigger steps. You don't want to bite off more than you can chew. Start small and build up to these goals. If, for example, you have a goal to run a 5K race yet you have not exercised in years, then start by jogging for two minutes on the first day and walking for another ten minutes. On day two, jog for three minutes and walk for another twelve, then slowly build up your jogging time till you are able to run the 5K. For any goal, find your pace by breaking it down into small steps to be taken on successive days or weeks.

- Avoid goals framed in a negative way, like *I'll be less angry* or *I will get upset less often*. Try to reformulate these goals in a positive way and as something that can be accomplished. For instance, you could make the goal *I will tell my son I love him once a day*, or you could set a goal like *I will attend a yoga class this week*.

With the online free tools at http://www.newharbinger.com/48336, you will find a Committed Action Worksheet you can use to record your goals, keeping track of the value that you want to work on, the specific goal that you have chosen to work on, the plan to achieve that goal, and the dates the goal was achieved.

This is a really good way to keep track of all the work you have accomplished. Be sure to periodically check your values assessment against the work you have done for committed action exercises. Does completing these activities help to close the gap between the value that is important to you and how closely you are living up to that value in your daily life?

In Amy's case, she reviewed her values again. She discovered that being a good parent and being healthy are really important values for her, but she wasn't satisfied with how much she had been living up to these values in her daily life. She rated both parenting and living a healthy life a

10, but she indicated that she rated her current effort in these areas a 7 for parenting and a 4 for healthy living. She decided to set some goals related to her values. Amy realized that instead of zoning out watching TV and eating sweets at the end of her workday, her time could be better spent with her daughter or improving her health. She decided to set goals of talking to her daughter for thirty minutes a day and walking in the park for thirty minutes a day. She planned to meet these goals for a week, then check on how she was feeling. This would help Amy figure out what would be a good substitute for unhealthy eating and also improve her quality of life.

Overcoming Barriers to Values-Based Living

It is normal to get stalled in reaching our goals. Our motivation to reach our goals can change, depending on our situation. Can you think of anything that may get in your way or stop you from achieving your goals? Cravings tend to be the usual suspects. Can you think of others? Barriers to achieving our goals are normal, and we have some good strategies to overcome them. We can label common barriers with the acronym FEAR, which stands for:

F = Fusion with thoughts

E = Evaluation of our experience

A = Avoidance

R = Reason-giving for our actions

Fusion means being too intertwined with the content in our heads. In chapter 6, we discussed how our minds become too focused on our cravings or other thoughts and emotions, and this fusion prevents our taking a step back and seeing the situation more clearly.

Evaluation of your experience can also be a substantial obstacle—like when we label particular things "good" or "bad" when these things aren't inherently good or bad. For instance, you might say to yourself, *My anxiety is so bad, there is no way that I can accomplish these goals.* As we discussed in chapter 6, anxiety doesn't necessarily have to be a bad thing. Anxiety serves an important purpose in our lives; we don't want to eliminate it. Another thought might be *If I go out, I am going to have a bad craving.* Cravings don't have to be "bad" either—they may not always be comfortable, but they are part of living with an addiction. Many people start to make a lot of progress on their goals once they move past needing to label cravings as bad things that they cannot have. It is okay to have cravings and still accomplish goals that have meaning for you.

Avoidance is a common obstacle to achieving goals. We may want to avoid spending more time with family because we are worried about getting into an argument that might trigger a craving. We might want to avoid going to a new yoga class because we would have to meet new people and we'll feel anxious about saying the wrong thing. Avoidance can keep us from pursuing meaningful activities that are important to us. Acceptance of and willingness to experience these obstacles can really help us regain control and fully engage in activities we've avoided.

Another common obstacle is *reason-giving.* We often give thoughts and emotions, including cravings, as reasons for not achieving important goals in our lives. For instance, we might tell ourselves *I am too anxious to start something new.* Participating in a new activity, like volunteering at a food bank or signing up for community theater, might cause us some anxiety, but that doesn't mean we can't participate. We might think *I can't go to the party, because it might make me feel more anxious and I'll want to drink.* This is an important thought to pay attention to. Think about other strategies that you can use that we discussed throughout the book that might be able to help you in this situation. Can you practice mindfulness to help you when your anxiety rises or you have a craving? Can you take a five-minute breather when you feel too much stress to practice mindful breathing and urge surfing? Coming up with a plan ahead of time can help you manage these experiences. But just because you feel anxious does not mean that you will have a drink. You don't always have to listen to what your cravings tell you to do. You are the decider.

We also have a good acronym for remembering actions to help you manage these common obstacles to committed action: ACT (the same name of this intervention we have been presenting in this book). It stands for:

A = Accept your reactions and be present.

C = Choose a valued direction.

T = Take action.

Accepting our reactions and being present is really helpful for overcoming our obstacles to committed action, especially when these obstacles are not within our control and we cannot change them. We can accept the presence of our cravings, thoughts, and emotions and make room for them in our lives. They will be here, whether we like them or not, so we might as well learn to make peace and live with them. This does not mean we like them or enjoy them or that we give in to them. We can accept our cravings as a component of being human that has been reinforced by our addictive behaviors. There may be times when we want to smoke, drink, use drugs, and eat addictive, unhealthy foods, and that's okay. Having the craving doesn't mean we have to act on the craving and give in to it. Instead, we can be more mindful and focused on the here and now. This way we acknowledge our cravings for what they are (usually just thoughts and sensations) and let them be, while turning our attention to the present and what is important to us.

To illustrate, consider what happens when you get bitten by a mosquito. A bump may appear on your skin that feels really itchy, and what is your urge? To scratch that itch. What happens if we do scratch it? The itch is caused by inflammation from a substance released by the mosquito, and scratching it increases the inflammation. Scratching in the moment feels good because it temporarily gives us some relief and distracts us from the itch we feel at the inflammation site, but if we continue to scratch, not only does the bite itch more, we also risk causing an infection. We cannot control feeling itchy when we get a mosquito bite. What we can control is whether we will scratch it or not. Acceptance in this case means making room for feeling the itch and choosing to not scratch it in the service of our skin's health.

The second step, choosing a valued direction, flows directly from being present. If we are mindful of what is important to us, we can turn our direction to our values and make a choice that is in line with what gives us meaning and purpose. We may feel anxious or have a strong craving. However, we can take a step back from those experiences and focus on our highly rated values, whether being physically healthy; supporting our spirituality; being a good partner, family member, parent, or friend; or taking pride in our work accomplishments. Megan worked with Joe, who quit smoking after a thirty-year habit. He often had strong cravings when he was faced with stress, even after being abstinent from smoking for a year. However, he held steadfast in his abstinence. How did he do this? He would remember that smoking resulted in a number of physical health issues, including cancer. When he had a strong craving, he would remember the toll that smoking had taken on his health, and it would help him choose not to pick cigarettes up again. During strong cravings, he would also remind himself of wanting to make his family proud. They, too, worried about his smoking, because it jeopardized his health. Focusing on his physical health and family helped him take a step back from his cravings and make a choice not to smoke that was consistent with his values.

The last step is to take action, which means accomplishing the goals we have been discussing and brainstorming. We can look at the values that are important to us and set goals in line with them. For instance, after Joe's strong cravings, he decided to set the following committed action goals:

- When I have a strong craving I will talk to my friend Charlie to stay abstinent.

- I will take a daily thirty-minute walk to improve my health.

- I will meditate for fifteen minutes every morning to balance my mood and stress and improve my health.

- I will visit my family once a week and eat dinner with them.

In the online free tools, we provided a Barriers to Committed Action worksheet. You can use this to help you think about what obstacles you may encounter when you start engaging in committed action. Take some time to list your barriers to living a valued life, and your plans for overcoming these obstacles. What small steps can you take in service of your values? This week, can you commit to a little step to close the gap between your values and how you have been living up to them?

Whenever you hit barriers to values-based living, it might be helpful to think about the following swamp metaphor (Hayes et al., 1999). Imagine that you are going out for a walk toward a beautiful, distant mountain. The mountain represents something important to you: your values. After a few minutes of walking, you look down and notice that your path is muddy and messy. Your shoes are getting dirty. You keep walking and find yourself knee-deep in a swamp. It's hard to walk; mud is getting into your shoes. You didn't know you would have to go through a swamp to get to where you want to go. You have a choice—you can either turn back or go through the swamp. If you turn back, you will never get to where you want to go— toward what is important to you. If you go through the swamp, you will feel uncomfortable for a time, but it will keep you on the path toward your values.

This metaphor represents what life often has to offer us: sometimes, when we move in the direction of our values, it can be difficult and messy. Sometimes we will feel uncomfortable. However, we go into the swamp not because we want to get muddy, but because it stands between where we are and where we really want to go in our lives.

Amy had been trying to take walks in the park for thirty minutes every day and taking thirty minutes a day to talk with her daughter. She was accomplishing her goals on some days, but not as often as she would like. She reviewed her obstacles. She found that on days that she felt really stressed out, she would tell herself, *This day was just horrible. I might as well eat some chocolate for a pick-me-up.* After she binged on chocolate, she felt even worse and gave up on committed action. She reviewed FEAR to better understand why she had difficulty engaging in her committed action activities on stressful days. She realized that she was evaluating the day as "all bad," which left her feeling like she wanted to give up on her goals. On stressful days, she decided to acknowledge her thoughts and do something else to manage the aftereffects of the stressful day. She decided to practice mindful breathing for a few quiet minutes during the workday and when she got home. She also practiced acceptance and defusion from thoughts and talked to herself in a more compassionate way: *You had a stressful day. Everyone would feel drained by this. Your body and mind need a break, and going for a walk would help you and is in line with your value of being healthier.* She realized that when she stopped struggling to make the stress go away, the stress was not such a big problem anymore. After she started practicing more mindfulness, particularly on her stressful days, she was able to complete her committed action activities, which gave her a lot of satisfaction. Interestingly, cravings for sweets did not seem so problematic anymore.

As we've discussed throughout this book, making changes takes practice and persistence. We choose to practice skills and be persistent in the face of barriers with the aim to further move our life toward where we would like to go and to live in a way that feels important and meaningful for us.

Choice Moment Aids

In this chapter we used the FEAR acronym to help us look out for common barriers to values-based living and the ACT acronym to designate steps we can take to setting values-based goals (as shown in the figure).

We again suggest using the Craving Choice Moment Diagram, found with the online free tools. If you print it out, it can serve as a reminder of your choices in each moment, with a visualization of your new skills readily at hand.

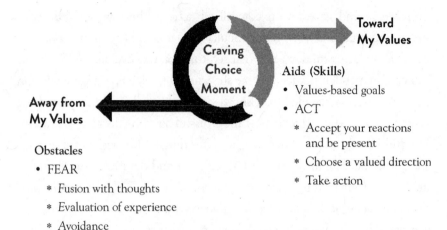

Toward My Values

Craving Choice Moment

Aids (Skills)
- Values-based goals
- ACT
  * Accept your reactions and be present
  * Choose a valued direction
  * Take action

Away from My Values

Obstacles
- FEAR
  * Fusion with thoughts
  * Evaluation of experience
  * Avoidance
  * Reason-giving

Bringing It All Together

- A value is the lighthouse in the storm. It is helpful for us to continually review our values and how we are living up to them.

- To reduce the void that often opens when we give up an addictive behavior, it helps to focus on committed action activities that are in line with our values.

- Committed action activities also help improve our quality of life and overall satisfaction.

- It is normal to experience obstacles to engaging in committed action activities. Common barriers form the acronym FEAR: **F**usion, **E**valuation, **A**voidance, and **R**eason-giving.

- A helpful way to overcome these barriers is to ACT: **A**ccept, **C**hoose a direction, and **T**ake action.

Bringing Our Learning to Life

This week, review your values and how you are living up to them. Pick a few committed action activities that can help reduce the gap between your values and how consistently you are living up to them, and schedule them in your week. If you are having a hard time engaging in these activities, think about what barriers may be in the way and work on a plan to overcome them.

In the next chapter, we will work on helping you develop a plan for dealing with common barriers to managing cravings.

CHAPTER 11

Dealing with Obstacles to Managing Cravings

Alex   *I am making a lot of progress with managing my drinking. I have sought professional help from a psychologist, and I have worked with my doctors to safely stop drinking. I am doing mindfulness practice regularly and learning to accept my cravings, thoughts, and emotions. I am being more compassionate with myself and am engaging in activities that matter to me. Overall, I am doing well. But some days are more challenging than others. Sometimes I see old friends who want me to go out drinking with them. At other times, I get so bored, and I start to romanticize drinking again. I know that drinking will not help me be a better family member or help me at work. But how do I deal with these situations and keep myself motivated?*

Alex's situation is very common. We might be making a great deal of progress in managing our cravings and improving our lives, yet there still are roadblocks that we need to learn to overcome. In this chapter, we will review some common obstacles to managing cravings and discuss how to work with them. We will also touch on the important issues of slips and relapses, and we'll help you take steps to move forward should these situations occur.

Common Challenges to Managing Cravings

On our journey to managing cravings better, we will inevitably encounter several challenges. We'll review these challenges and provide suggestions for overcoming them.

Being in an Environment That Supports Substance Use

We can sometimes find ourselves in situations where we are surrounded by very powerful cues to use. For instance, we could find ourselves at a party where there is a lot of drinking, drug use, or junk food. We may walk into a group of people who are smoking. We have to be in tune with ourselves to know whether we can manage these situations well. If necessary, we can mindfully check in with our bodies, thoughts, and emotions and see what is happening for ourselves. If you inadvertently find yourself among a lot of people engaging in addictive behaviors or you are in a place that might lead to your using when you do not want to, it is okay to *leave* that situation. Don't worry about offending anyone or any other consequences. You can have compassion for yourself in this situation and do what you think is best. Often that means leaving a situation that would support addictive behaviors. In such situations you have a choice: stay or leave. Which choice is in line with your values?

Boredom

Boredom is a common trigger for cravings. When we have time on our hands, cravings tend to be more frequent. Before we started working on new strategies for managing cravings, you likely filled your time with using substances like food, cigarettes, alcohol, and drugs. Now that you aren't using substances to fill that space, boredom can trigger cravings. When facing this situation, we suggest reviewing the previous chapter's section on committed action. Fill up your life with other activities that bring meaning to your life. If you feel bored, that's okay. Boredom is a normal human experience. If you experience a craving when you are bored, that's okay, that's what your mind comes up with to relieve the boredom. But it doesn't mean that you must listen to your mind and give in to that craving. Instead, you can turn to what is important to you and engage in a committed action activity that brings you satisfaction and joy. You can learn to fill up your time with activities like reading, meditating, spending time with family or friends, hiking, and new hobbies. Accepting the presence of cravings when you get bored and then engaging in activities that bring you meaning can give you more satisfaction with life. This may also be a good opportunity to meet new people, join a new group, and explore more about what you like and want to commit to in your life.

Substituting One Addictive Behavior for Another

It is common to turn to familiar old ways we know help us cope with the world. When it comes to addictive behaviors, it is really common to substitute one addictive behavior for another. We have worked with people recovering from addictions for more than fifteen years. When helping people to recover from addictions, Megan commonly sees people start to eat more or smoke more when they have given up another type of addiction, such as drugs or alcohol. For example, one person started to substitute candy bars for cigarettes. Others substituted soda for their addictions. It wasn't uncommon to hear about beautiful dreams of exotic foods, like gigantic enchiladas! Our minds are accustomed to engaging in addictive behaviors, so it can take time to break out of the habit of using substances to make us feel good in the moment. It is particularly helpful for us to be aware of what we are doing so we can substitute healthier behaviors for harmful addictions. Exercise can release the same types of feel-good endorphins that we get from other addictions (talk with your health care provider before engaging in any new exercise routine you're unaccustomed to). Substituting other pleasant activities can also give us the same satisfaction that we were getting from harmful addictions—if not more. Indeed, research on oxytocin (a feel-good hormone) shows it's released when we give ourselves or someone else a loving hug. Go ahead and try it—give yourself a big hug right now and notice how your body feels.

Experiencing Physical Pain

Physical pain and cravings are very closely tied. When we are in pain, we often look for some relief. It is common to reach for a substance, like food, cigarettes, alcohol, and drugs to provide temporary relief from the pain. If you are in recovery from an addiction and are in pain (like recovering from an accident or surgery), you may also be prescribed pain medication with the potential for addiction. This can be a tricky situation if you have a tendency for addictive behaviors. It is important to discuss your history with your doctor, particularly if you have a prior history of problematic alcohol and drug use. Prescription opioid pain medications can put you at potential risk of developing a new addiction or relapsing on opioids if you have a prior history. Work with your doctor on your pain-management needs, discuss an effective plan for you, and consider non-pharmacological pain-management methods that could also help. The approach you have been learning in this book has also demonstrated empirical effectiveness in managing pain. You can use the same techniques in this book to help with any pain, given that pain is just another sensation, as is craving.

Not Having Enough Support or Not Having Helpful Support

When you are managing cravings and addictive behaviors, it is really helpful to have a support system that can cheer you on during challenging times. It can be hard to change when we don't have other people's support to help us. It can be especially difficult if your support system is full of people who encourage addictive behaviors; these people can be powerful triggers for you. It is hard to give up old friends who are encouraging us to go back into our old, more harmful ways. Everyone needs support, so not having helpful support around you can be a challenge. This is an opportunity to develop a new social support system. It will be helpful to think about people in your life who can help encourage you and keep you on track. Consider strengthening connections to people who can talk you through a difficult craving and remind you why you are committed to changing your approach to your cravings and addictive behaviors. Relying on others for support when you are managing an addiction is one of the most important things you can do to continue on your recovery journey. We devoted a whole chapter to this important topic; see chapter 12 for more about building a support system.

Managing Slips and Relapses

Slips and relapses are common in the recovery from substances. We rarely get things right the first time, and that also goes for managing cravings. We'll discuss how to manage slips and relapses so we can continue to focus on living a values-based life.

How to Manage a Slip

Slips happen. A slip is a brief return to substance use, particularly smoking, alcohol, and drug use, but not a return to full use. We can slip with eating unhealthy food as well. Cravings can sometimes be powerful and get the better of us. This does not have to mean we are back to our old ways. How we respond to a slip can make the difference between going back to how we used to manage cravings or continuing to move in a values-driven direction.

Let's review how we usually feel when we slip and give in to our cravings after we have been trying to change the way we respond to them. It is common to put ourselves down. We might think *I've failed, I'm weak,* or *I've let down everyone I care about.* You may experience a flood of different emotions. You may be angry with yourself. You may feel down, or embarrassed, or guilty. In addition, you might start to lose hope and motivation for changing. You might believe that you will never kick your addiction or ever be able to manage cravings more effectively.

These reactions are normal. We want you to be aware of them, because being aware might help prevent you from giving up completely. In our experience, most people slip. Nobody is perfect, and there are going to be times when we get partway through the swamp and want to turn back; we may even take a few steps back. That doesn't mean that you can't continue on your journey to what is important to you.

If we find ourselves in this situation, what do we do? First, we can choose to take a few breaths and step back from our predicament. This is a choice moment, and we can choose to follow what is important to us and continue our effort to stop smoking, bingeing, drinking, or using drugs, even though we just had a slip. If we're in a situation where an external trigger is present, it's a good idea to leave the situation. For instance, if you are in a bar, you can leave the bar. If you are in a group of people smoking, you can leave the group. If you are reacting to an internal trigger, like dealing with stress, you will have to handle this situation differently. Leaving this situation may not be an option, yet you have in your hands a whole book full of techniques on how to manage the situation. When internal triggers show up, recognize and name them (you can jokingly say, *Hello, my old friend*). Notice mindfully what you are thinking and feeling in this moment (in the here and now). Use defusion and acceptance techniques to make room for those thoughts and feelings. Perhaps try urge surfing or mindful breathing to return your attention to the present.

Remember, in this situation, you do not have to listen to what your mind is telling you. You have not failed. You are not weak. There is nothing in this situation that defines you that way. Your mind will come up with all sorts of labels—these do not represent who you are. These thoughts are just clouds moving past you—you are the sky and are not defined by these passing clouds. Recognize that you are more than your thoughts and feelings and extend some loving-kindness to yourself and this experience you are having. What you need to do now is to get in touch with what is important to you. Why did you commit to managing your cravings differently? Was it to have better health? Was it to be a better parent, friend, family member, or partner? You can think about what is important and recommit to managing your addictions more effectively and getting back on track. You can remind yourself, *I want to quit* [the addictive substance] *because* [your reasons].

It can help if you recognize that this slip was an important learning experience. If you have a slip, it indicates that you have identified a situation that you need to plan around. After all, you learned how to smoke, drink, binge, and use drugs. You weren't born doing these things—you learned to include these behaviors in your life. You will have to be compassionate with yourself and recognize that you need to learn how to stop giving in to cravings and addictions. You also need to remember all of the hard work that you have put in so far and commit to not giving up.

The period of time after you have a slip is a good opportunity to think about the situation in which you experienced the craving. You can choose to put a plan together to learn how to cope with this situation more effectively. What strategies from the past few chapters can you use to manage this situation now? If this situation happens again, what can you do to handle it? If you are seeking additional support from counselors or other providers, this might be a good time to talk to them (see chapter 12 for when and how to seek out professional help). It is okay to accept your reactions to your slip while reminding yourself of why you can handle this situation differently in the future. Then you can direct your attention to your next choice and make it be about moving in the direction of your values.

High-Risk Situations for Relapse

In contrast to a slip, which is a singular, short-term event, relapsing means going fully back to using a substance for a period of time. It can be particularly helpful for us to understand what situations will place us at high risk of relapse so that we can be more aware of these situations and plan ahead. Let's review some common situations that can lead to relapse.

FEELING OVERCONFIDENT OR COMPLACENT

It is important to be confident about managing cravings, but not overconfident. You may need to take note of certain thoughts; for instance, *One drink can't hurt,* or *I know I can handle one cigarette.* We might feel complacent in our recovery and think that we have permanent control over our cravings. After all, we have been doing a great job for a while, so why not treat ourselves? This is an important chain of thoughts to take a step back from and observe. It's a good time to see if there are other thoughts and emotions we might have been setting aside that we haven't dealt with effectively, leading us to entertain having "one" for "old time's sake." Is boredom a trigger? It helps to regularly check in on your thoughts and emotions with the mindfulness you've been cultivating. It is also important to review your values to remind yourself why you've committed yourself to changing how you approach cravings and addictions. Reviewing your values can help you to recommit and recognize what you have to lose if you have "just one"—and what you have to gain when you focus on what is important to you.

HIGH LEVELS OF STRESS

Very stressful situations or experiencing strong emotions can present a high-risk situation for relapse. One very common reason people give for relapse is stress. As we've discussed, it is possible to experience stress and strong emotions and still manage cravings effectively. Just because a situation is challenging or you feel a particular way (anger, anxiety, feeling low, having pain) does not mean you must give in to cravings. However, hearing bad news, going through a crisis, or experiencing financial problems are examples of challenging situations that give rise to strong cravings that can lead to relapse.

Megan once worked with someone who found himself very anxious after hearing about the loss of his father, and he had strong cravings to drink. Experiencing stress and strong emotions is part of being human, and it is normal to have cravings in these situations. How we manage those cravings can make all the difference. First, it is important to be compassionate with ourselves in these situations and recognize the stressful situation we are in. Then break down the situation's challenges into small steps that are not overwhelming. Can you call someone for support? Can you take a walk to get some distance from the stressful situation? Can you do a five-minute mindfulness exercise to observe your thoughts and feelings and ride out the urge to use? It helps to prepare yourself for these situations during a relatively uneventful, normal time in your life. Having a crisis-management coping plan prepared can help you during stressful times. Remember, this too shall pass, and you will be proud of yourself for managing the stress without relying on a substance to "help" you.

CONFLICT WITH OTHERS

Conflicts with others commonly lead to strong cravings and relapse. Relationship problems and fights with others can make anger rise quickly, and sometimes in these situations we act impulsively and binge, smoke, drink, or use drugs. We may even have vengeful thoughts, like *This will show them*, if we give in to cravings—potentially trying to hurt another person by relapsing on a substance. Megan worked with someone who had very strong cravings when he got into arguments with his roommates—cravings to both drink and smoke. These thoughts led him to relapse, which only left him feeling bad about himself. Tired of this pattern, he decided to change his approach. Now when he gets into arguments, he leaves the room, takes a break, and mindfully breathes. He mindfully watches his angry thoughts float by while he pays attention to his breath. He also takes this time to remember why he doesn't drink or smoke anymore. He wants to make his family proud and have better health. After a few minutes, he is ready to reengage with his roommates to resolve the argument and move past the issue that was causing him anger.

PLEASANT TIMES WITH OTHERS

Yet another high-risk situation for relapse is having a pleasant time with others. How can feeling good and enjoying the company of others lead to relapse? Imagine that it is a sports championship event and your favorite team is playing. You are having a good time with your friends. Then a friend opens up a beer, because drinking would make this event even more enjoyable. In this situation it is common to think, *Well, I could just have one this time, because we're all having a good time, and I'll get back on track tomorrow.* Megan works in New England, home of the New England Patriots who won the Super Bowl six times between 2002 and 2019. Whenever the Patriots were in the Super Bowl, she knew she'd be hearing from a few people who had slips and relapses due to the event. Now, it is great to have an enjoyable time with friends and family. We should do this as much as we can. But we also need to consider whether there will be any triggers for cravings at those events that we need to plan for, and what action plan we could prepare in case we experience a strong craving.

Managing Relapse

If you relapse, you are not alone. For those who have committed to abstinence from smoking, drinking, or using drugs, relapse is always a possibility. This is a critical point at which to think about what is important to you and decide whether you want to recommit to a healthier, more fulfilling life by stopping your substance use. Relapsing is not the end; it can be the point of a new beginning, as you always have a choice of how to behave in this moment. Remember, no one can change the past or the future; we can only choose how to behave in the present. A relapse is also a signal of emotional pain that needs to be dealt with more effectively, so we likely need more support (see chapter 12 for seeking professional help).

If you have relapsed to drinking or using drugs, it's vitally important to consider whether professional help is needed. In the beginning of this book we encouraged you to seek professional help if you have a long-standing addiction to alcohol or drugs, because you might need to go through a detoxification and rehabilitation process. We also encourage seeking help for renewing your commitment to quitting substance use after a relapse. Detox from alcohol, opiates, and benzodiazepine use can be dangerous, even life-threatening. So seek professional help once you make the important decision to quit again, and work with your providers to do detox safely.

After recommitment to abstinence, we can review the same steps outlined in managing slips to help you move forward. Some individuals that Maria has worked with find it easier to commit to a short period of time rather than to forever, as that may seem like a huge mountain to climb all at once. So we commit to being abstinent in each moment and connect with our values each time we face a choice moment and actively choose to be abstinent. This is your life, so choose the way that works for you. If setting a long-term plan of abstinence is helpful, do that. If instead you want to set short-term goals, take it a step at a time.

When a slip or relapse happens, we may feel guilt and anger at ourselves. This is a completely normal and expected reaction. Judging or beating yourself up will not help you move in a healthier direction. In fact, you can learn a lot from relapsing. Reviewing what led to relapse can help inform the next steps to a sustained recovery. It is helpful to accept and acknowledge mistakes, learn from the situation, and move on a path toward your values.

When we find ourselves in a difficult situation, a slip or a relapse, one way to remember what we can do based on the skills we learned in this book is summarized in the acronym STOP (Harris, 2009):

- Slow down

- Take note

- Open up

- Pursue valued actions

Let's walk through these four elements.

Slow down. If we have a long learning history of behaving in a certain way (such as relying on using, smoking, unhealthy food, or alcohol), when faced with a craving or a difficult situation we are likely to go into autopilot mode and act impulsively. Slowing down helps us pause to be able to consider and use our skills. We can slow down by taking a few mindful breaths—we recommend five. Maria calls this *pentadaktylos* breathing (Greek for "five fingers"). Use your fingers to help you connect to the moment and to your breath. Use your right-hand index finger to touch the base of your left thumb. Inhale, and as you do, draw your index finger over your thumb and up to its top. Exhale and draw the index finger down the other side of your thumb. Continue with the right index finger until you go through all of your five fingers and have taken five mindful breaths.

Take note is about observing what shows up. Observe your thoughts, emotions, and bodily sensations, nonjudgmentally. Name them if you want, and notice where you are experiencing them within you; for example, *Here is a craving, and I feel it in my stomach.*

Open up or accept whatever thoughts, emotions, sensations, memories, urges, or cravings you have. Make room and let these experiences flow like the leaves falling in the stream or the clouds in the sky. Use any of the defusion, acceptance, and mindfulness skills we have learned to make room and allow these internal events to exist without judgment or struggle.

Pursue valued actions. This is your choice moment, and you can connect with your choices for how you want to behave next. Connect with your values and let them guide your choice of action.

Choice Moment Aids

In this chapter we identified common challenges to managing cravings for the long hall and in high-risk situations for relapse. We discussed how we can manage slips and prevent relapse. The choice moment in this figure summarizes this information. Make sure to add these tools for managing slips and preventing relapse to your Craving Choice Moment Diagram (from the online free tools). Keep a printout of this diagram so that you have it when you need it at choice moment crossroads.

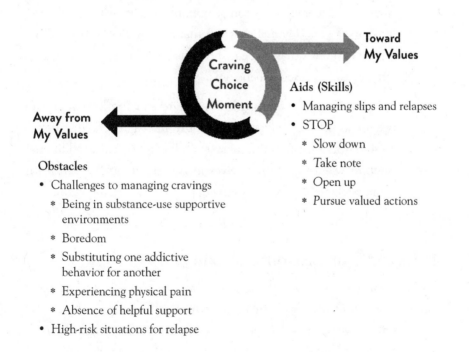

Toward My Values

Craving Choice Moment

Aids (Skills)
- Managing slips and relapses
- STOP
  * Slow down
  * Take note
  * Open up
  * Pursue valued actions

Away from My Values

Obstacles
- Challenges to managing cravings
  * Being in substance-use supportive environments
  * Boredom
  * Substituting one addictive behavior for another
  * Experiencing physical pain
  * Absence of helpful support
- High-risk situations for relapse

Bringing It All Together

- Some common obstacles to managing addictions include finding yourself in an environment that supports addictive behaviors, feeling bored, substituting one addiction for another, experiencing physical pain, and not having enough support. Be aware of these common obstacles and make a plan for overcoming them using the strategies outlined here.

- Slips are a common and normal part of experiencing cravings and addictions. How we manage the slip is a key difference between a full relapse and continuing to move in the direction of our values.

- Be aware of several high-risk situations for relapse, including feeling overconfident about managing cravings, high levels of stress and experiencing strong emotions, conflict with others, and enjoying pleasant activities with other people. Developing a game plan for these situations can help sustain progress in managing cravings and addictive behaviors.

- Finally, if we relapse, this is not a failure and a reflection of who we are as people. We can recommit to managing cravings better and to stop using harmful substances. It can help to get additional support when we find ourselves in this situation. We can learn from a relapse and keep moving in a values-driven direction.

Bringing Our Learning to Life

Over the next week, think about these common obstacles to managing cravings. If you identify with them, add them to your list of triggers for cravings and develop an action plan for them. Think about high-risk situations for relapse, and develop an action plan for those as well.

We talked a lot in this chapter about finding support for managing cravings and addictive behaviors. In the next chapter, we will discuss this in more detail.

CHAPTER 12

Getting Support for Managing Cravings

Alex   *Now that I've stopped drinking, I sometimes feel alone. I used to go out drinking with my buddies at bars or watch sports and drink with them. Being around them in these situations is going to risk my sobriety. I know I will have strong cravings if I go back to my old routines with them. The problem is, these friends don't recognize that drinking is such as problem for me. They just want me to give up on my sobriety and hang out like old times. Sometimes I really feel like I want to. But I've decided to commit to a better way of life. I have two friends who quit drinking themselves, and they really understand what I am going through. They have been there for me when I've had tough cravings. They have helped remind me of what's really important to me and that giving up on my sobriety is not going to help my health, relationships with family members, or my work. I'm grateful for their support—and I am glad to have them by my side while I am learning to manage my cravings for alcohol.*

Having a helpful support network when you are dealing with cravings is one of the most important things you can do to stay on your path to a healthier and better life. In fact, many of us place relationships, including those with family and friends, high on our values list. Social support can:

- Buffer us from the effects of stress

- Help us improve our ability to cope with life events

- Talk us through challenging cravings

- Encourage us to follow our values

- Promote good health and positive life choices

- Help us to adhere to our committed action plans

We humans are social animals; we do better when we are closely connected with others. Giving social support ourselves leads to emotional, physical, and social benefits for us.

A plethora of research documents the benefits of social support and how, overall as humans, we flourish when we are in secure and close relationships (Taylor, 2011). Research also confirms that it is more the quality than the quantity of relationships that is important, especially as we age (Carmichael, Reis, & Duberstein, 2015). So we do not necessarily need lots of friends, as having one or two close relationships can provide us with all the benefits just listed. Yet we find that sometimes if individuals have only one close relationship, they expect it to fulfill all their needs; this may create problems, as one person may not be able to live up to this. Amy, for example, thought that her husband should fulfill all her romantic, friendship, and activity needs, yet he kept falling short. He did not care about some of her interests—he preferred watching football to romantic comedy or philosophical movies, and he did not particularly enjoy discussing the meaning of films after watching them. This left Amy feeling dissatisfied and unsupported in the relationship and often drove her to overeat. When Amy realized that maybe her husband did not have to fulfill all these needs, she found new sources of support. She signed up for a "Friends of Cinema" group, where she met new friends with whom to watch and discuss films together.

So who can you go to when you need help with cravings? Who can you rely on?

Identifying Helpful Sources of Support

Helpful supports are people who are looking out for our best interests. We may already know several helpful people to call if we are having tough cravings. They can talk us through these situations and remind us of what's important, helping us take a step back from our thoughts and emotions, practice acceptance of a craving, and move in our valued direction. Support can come in many different forms. Even people who are still engaging in addictive behaviors can be important supports if they are standing up for what's important to us. In Megan's work with people recovering from substance use disorders, she has heard about several friends who refused to give cigarettes, alcohol, or drugs to her client even when asked, because they wanted their friend to stay on their path to recovery and a better life. These people recognized that even if they were not ready to take steps in managing their own cravings and addictive behaviors more effectively, they did not want to jeopardize someone else.

If you are having trouble identifying who a good support might be, that's completely normal! Sometimes when we give up an addiction, our social support system needs to change. Who is going to have our back?

A helpful supporter will listen to us nonjudgmentally. They will encourage us to do our best and follow our values, and check in with us to see how we are doing. A helpful supporter is *not* someone who will nag us. Some people think they are providing support by nagging, but this actually demotivates many of us. You want supporters who will not be overly critical. Also consider your candidates' honesty, sincerity, reliability, responsibility, and ability to follow through on what they say. But recognize that no one is perfect. Having overly rigid rules for people will impede your progress in lining up support. Potential great supporters will have their own stresses to deal with, and for us to be a helpful support to *them*, we must be willing to provide the same nonjudgmental attitude and support that they offer us.

Here is a checklist of characteristics to look for in a helpful supporter:

Characteristic	Yes	No
Do they listen to you?		
Do they give helpful advice?		
Are they trustworthy?		

Characteristic	Yes	No
Are they honest?		
Are they reliable?		
Are they responsible?		
Can you share both good and bad news with them?		
Do they stand up for you?		
Do they have your best interests in mind: your sobriety and your choices for living a values-driven life?		
Does your intuition (gut) tell you that they are there for you?		

With these characteristics in mind, who are helpful supports in your life? Are there family members, friends, coworkers, or neighbors you can count on for support with your cravings? That's wonderful! It is helpful to know that we have people to rely on when the going gets tough. But what if we do not yet have such helpful people in our lives?

Building a Social Support Network

It's essential to have people available who support you in managing cravings and achieving your values-based goals. Here are some ways to build or expand your social support network to help you achieve success.

Meeting New People

To build or expand a social support network, your first step will likely be to meet new people. You will have to put yourself in situations where you will be around others, including strangers. To find people you might have something in common with, look to places where you might have that something in common. Volunteering, community activities, houses of worship, and recreational groups are some ideas for meeting someone who we might share something in common with.

Jeff, whom we met in an earlier chapter, wanted to build a strong social support network. He needed to develop healthier friendships because his old friends were still using drugs and didn't recognize how harmful drugs had been to Jeff—or themselves. He joined a local yoga class and a hiking group. These activities enabled him to meet some new people, and he used the criteria just provided to evaluate whether a person might be someone he would like get to know better. He found a couple of people he thought he would get along with and introduced himself. When the conversation went well, he invited them to get coffee and talk some more. He then arranged more activities with them, and gradually new friendships blossomed. Jeff had to expand his comfort zone to engage in new activities and to approach and talk to others. He acted with willingness, as he recognized that meeting new people aligned with the valued-living path he wanted to be on. These new friendships helped Jeff gain support for his new way of managing his cravings and addictive behaviors.

Listening

To develop new relationships with others, it is important to be a good listener yourself and be there for them in times of need. Relationships are a two-way street: to receive support, we need to give support. Being a good listener makes people feel good; they perceive that we really care and feel that we are connected.

Megan once went to a seminar where the speaker talked about being in a conversation with the Dalai Lama. The speaker said that his ability to listen was incredible—he made her feel as if she was the only person in a large room full of people. We can all work on being as good at listening as the Dalai Lama! The Dalai Lama was practicing mindful listening, which involves being fully present when you are interacting with other people. It is common for us to have an ongoing commentary in our minds while we talk to people—what tasks we have to complete, our weekend plans, or recent news from a colleague. Often we don't hear the entire content of a conversation because we are paying attention to something else in our minds. When we listen mindfully, we give our full attention to what the other person is saying, fully hearing and processing their words. We demonstrate genuine interest in the topic by making eye contact, smiling, and nodding. People can sense when they are truly being heard. Here are some more guidelines for mindful listening:

- **Be present.** Put all your attention on what the person is saying. As soon as you realize your mind is wandering, bring your mind back to the conversation at hand. If judgments appear, recognize them and return to the speaker. Attend to the voice of the person, its pitch, its rhythm. Notice the person's body language and the movement of their mouth. Engage with their words and try to comprehend the content nonjudgmentally.

- **Listen with empathy.** "Empathy" is defined as the ability to understand and share the feelings of another. This means giving people room to share their experiences, thoughts, and feelings, without breaking in, correcting them, or giving advice. Notice your urge to respond in some of these ways, and choose to say something or act based not on what your mind says but on your commitment to be an active, empathetic listener.

- **Reflect back to the other person what they are saying.** This is validating and helps the person know that you've heard them. It allows them to correct any misconceptions, which helps improve communication and understanding. To reflect, you can use a simple formula of "You feel/felt X when Y happened." Mindful reflection sounds like this:

  - You have expressed that you think…

  - It seems like or sounds like you experienced…

  - I hear you say that you need…

- **Be aware of your own reactions.** It is helpful to clue in to how you are feeling, because it can influence your reactions to the other person. You can watch your reactions as they happen, and check to see if these might be interfering with your ability to non-judgmentally listen to the person in front of you.

Having Open and Honest Communication

For a helpful, supportive relationship, it is imperative to be open and honest and expect the same from others. Helpful supports will accept hearing about our thoughts and feelings. We can be open without being critical. If we have conflicts, we can listen mindfully and allow the other person to respond. Our minds can easily assume bad motives, when often misunderstandings and hurt feelings are unintentional.

Being Patient

We need to be patient with those who are learning how to be supportive or building the skills to learn how to help. They may need a little more information, guidance from us, and time to learn how to best support us.

Communicating Assertively

Being assertive means expressing your needs in a manner that helps others understand and increases the likelihood they will support you. It does not mean always getting your way. Again, you'll need to distinguish between what you control (your behavior) and what is not in your control (others' behavior). Assertive communication involves three simple steps:

1. Present the situation you would like to discuss or the problem to be solved in a matter-of-fact way, as if describing a traffic incident you just observed. This involves presenting the situation without pointing fingers or blaming anyone. The point is to help the other person hear your perspective without them getting into a defensive mode or building a wall to protect themselves from a seeming attack. (An example follows to demonstrate this step.)

2. Express how the situation (not the other person) makes you feel. Talking about feelings is important; when we humans hear others express their emotions, we tend to tune in and be more empathetic.

3. State clearly and directly what you want in this situation, or if there is not one specific thing you want to ask for, invite discussion to find the best solution for each person involved.

For example, Amy wanted to express to her husband how she was feeling unsupported in her efforts to eat healthier, as the other family members kept bringing junk food into the house. Amy had this conversation with her husband, using the assertiveness formula:

1. As you know, I have been trying to eat a healthier diet, and it becomes hard to make healthy choices when junk food is regularly brought into our house.

2. This makes me feel unsupported, disappointed, and angry.

3. I would ask that we limit ordering junk food for dinner to twice per week.

Amy was impressed when her husband listened and responded empathetically that he had not realized how hard this was for her and that he wanted to support her. Together they agreed on dinner plans for each week and limited takeout fast food to once per week.

This way of communicating is different from being aggressive (stating only your needs and trying to get your way no matter what) or being passive (not expressing your needs, bottling up your feelings). You may notice that being assertive is about expressing your feelings and needs in a way that the other person will listen to, while being attentive to balancing your needs with those of the other person. For this to work better, ensure that your request is couched as a "do" rather than a "do not." Amy asked that they order takeout only two times a week, rather than state that they *should not* order takeout nightly. Being assertive takes practice, especially if this is not the way you're used to communicating with others. Plan ahead for the conversation you would like to have, so you do not struggle to find the right words during the conversation. Through practice, this way of communicating will become easier for you to carry out.

Balancing Their Needs with Your Needs

It can be easy to get lost in a relationship and to try to be whatever the other person wants. For healthy relationships to develop, we have to balance someone else's needs with our own. Being everything to someone else can cause us to neglect ourselves. Cravings and addictive behaviors can be difficult to manage if we don't give ourselves enough space and time to focus on what we need. Megan worked with Mary, who gave up alcohol. In her recovery, she developed a meaningful, supportive relationship with Brad. Everything was going really well with Brad for a while, but she devoted all of her time to him and his needs. She started to experience very strong cravings. When she thought about why this was the case, she realized that she was putting off going to many activities that she found meaningful—going to church, meditation, and taking art classes. She realized that she needed to take care of her needs too—this not only helped her manage her cravings better, but it made her a better partner to Brad.

Using Social Supports for Help in Managing Cravings

Ask for help. When you're having a tough time with cravings, it can be helpful to call a friend or family member. You can talk to them about what is on your mind, what is important to you, and why what you crave—bingeing, smoking, drinking, or using drugs—is not helpful or consistent with your values. You can bring up the concerns that might be triggering your cravings and see if they can help you work through the situation. Use your assertive communication techniques to assist you when asking for help.

Brainstorm your craving game plan. When having a craving, talk to friends and family about what you could do as an alternative to giving in to the craving. Talking to supportive, caring others can be another tool for your craving management toolbox. You can ask your supportive social network to help you brainstorm ideas for committed action activities that contribute to values-based living.

Ask for encouragement. When we have tough cravings, thoughts, and emotions, it can really be helpful to turn to our supports for encouragement. They can give us a boost, let us know we are not alone, and remind us of how far we have come in managing cravings and improving our lives. If you lose perspective on how far you have come, your supports can often point out all the positive changes you've made.

Partner for committed action. Some of our more meaningful committed action activities happen with others. Look at the list of activities in chapter 10; many of these are social. So grab a friend and join a book club, or attend a class with a support; go the gym or concert with a friend or family member. It can be easier to commit to committed action when you have someone else there to encourage you.

Dealing with Unhelpful Supports

When we are surrounded by people who are engaging in addictive behaviors—eating unhealthy food, smoking, drinking alcohol, or using drugs—there is often pressure to do the same. It can come directly from the people we are with who tell us that it's okay to have a drink or a cigarette. Or it can come from just being in their presence and wanting to fit in. Megan works in a setting where it had been the norm for people to smoke on their breaks. People wanting to quit smoking would often say that they wanted to give up cigarettes but felt like they needed to smoke to be liked and to be accepted by the group. A lot of socializing happened in this smoking group, and it was difficult to be on the outside. We may go along with substance use to avoid being made fun of and to feel like we are being rebellious. These can be substantial challenges to our goals of managing cravings and addictive behaviors.

Some people are going to be fantastic supports for us in managing cravings. A really helpful support wants what is best for us. But there are also going to be people, particularly people who are using substances themselves, who want us to go back to using. Maybe our success in managing cravings and addictive behaviors threatens them. They may not be ready to tackle their addictions themselves, and our use justifies their use. For instance, a friend may want us to drink because he's been our drinking buddy for years. Now that we're ready to move on from problematic drinking, he's afraid of losing the friendship and having to reflect on his own alcohol use. He may want us to drink so he won't feel awkward about his drinking too. However, his use does not have to affect our use. This person may be a good friend in many other respects, but his addiction is preventing him from being a good friend to us in this particular situation.

Sometimes a friend or family member encourages us to use because they are afraid of what will happen if we stop using. For instance, when someone quits smoking, they commonly feel irritable and grouchy in the first few days. This is only temporary and it will pass. However, sometimes family members don't like to deal with someone who is more on edge and might be a little short with them. They might tell the new nonsmoker to have a cigarette to calm down. It's tempting to give in to cravings and smoke simply to avoid friction.

If we find ourselves in these situations, it is really important to have a plan for managing them. It is important for us to stand up for our decision to not engage in our addictive behavior, like smoking, drinking, or using drugs. We've committed to managing cravings and addictions differently, because engaging in them wasn't helping us to get to where we want to be.

There are many strategies for responding to people who encourage us to use:

- Give them a straightforward "No thanks." For example, if someone offers you a cigarette you could say, "No thanks. I don't smoke." Be confident and clear, and make eye contact to communicate your position.

- If people keep insisting, repeat your response. You don't have to explain yourself. Explaining yourself may become a trap: you give one reason, the person finds a way to counter that reason, and it becomes all the harder to resist a craving.

- Suggest another activity that won't lead to cravings, ask friends for support, or leave the situation entirely. It can be really helpful to practice your response to these situations in advance. Try role-playing different responses to situations like these:

- "Just have another slice of cake. Life is too short to worry about it."

- "You are so grouchy. You might as well have a cigarette."

- "Just one drink isn't going to hurt you."

Friends, family members, or others may get angry or ridicule us for not engaging in addictive behaviors. They may be dealing with their own thoughts and feelings and relying on substances to make them "feel" better. They are on their own journey of managing cravings and addictive behaviors, and only they can make those decisions for themselves. If we feel shamed or hurt in this situation, this is completely normal. People we love, care for, and respect are trying to convince us to engage in unhealthy behaviors that are not consistent with what is important for us. In these situations, it is essential to stay connected with our values, the reasons we have given up unhealthy addictions and want to manage our cravings differently.

What are your reasons for not listening when people encourage you to engage in unhealthy addictions? Do you value your independence, freedom, or physical and mental health? You value relationships, but is this a healthy relationship? Would a true friend want you to do something that is not in your best interest? Think of the airline safety talk: if oxygen masks drop down, you should put on your own before helping someone else to put on theirs. Similarly, when someone else is on their own recovery journey, they deserve compassion, but you need to take care of yourself first (put on your own oxygen mask).

When it comes to dealing with unhelpful supports, we have the following choices:

- Leave a toxic environment or relationship.

- Change what you *can* change (such as the way you talk or behave toward others), accepting that this does not mean they will also change.

- Accept what you *cannot* change, and use the skills learned in this book to act based on what you value.

There is, of course, one more thing you can do: give in to the craving and fall back into old habits. We hope you will not choose this last option, but will use your skills to choose one of the alternatives that will allow you to continue along your valued-living path.

When and How to Seek Professional Help

Many cravings can be managed on your own, as you have been learning here. But if you are having a hard time applying the skills proposed here or dealing with cravings on your own, we encourage you to seek out professional help. For cravings for unhealthy food, counselors and support groups can offer us ideas and assistance for managing them beyond our own best-laid plans. Smoking-cessation counseling, particularly if we have tried to quit several times on our own, can also help us brainstorm ideas and a new quitting plan. Smoking-cessation medications can help ease withdrawal symptoms and free us to work on coping more effectively with other aspects of our cravings (that is, our internal and external triggers). It's always a good idea to seek out professional help for dealing with problematic alcohol and drug use, since there can be more serious issues of withdrawal, particularly with alcohol, opiate, and benzodiazepine use. In such situations, we may need medical detox to safely stop using these substances. And it is often necessary and advisable to seek professional help for managing serious addictions to drugs like cocaine, marijuana, and stimulants.

We recommend seeking professional help for an addiction if you:

- Need more and more of a substance to get the same effect it once had.

- Experience withdrawal symptoms from a substance when you stop using it.

- Need to use a substance to stop withdrawal symptoms.

- Continue to use even though it makes you feel sick or impairs your mental health.

- Find it is interfering with relationships.

- Find it is interfering with work.

- Are not taking care of yourself.

- Get angry with others when they ask about your use of substances.

- Deny that you have a problem.

We often want to handle these situations alone, thinking that we can just take care of it ourselves, or we are too embarrassed to seek help. But every one of us needs help from others at some time and in one form or another. Accepting help is not a sign of weakness or failure. It's a sign that you are compassionate with yourself and are doing what it takes to move in the direction of your values.

Professional help for managing cravings and addictions offers these benefits:

- We can learn a lot about ourselves by talking to a professional who knows about cravings and addictions.

- For some addictions, like those for nicotine, alcohol, and drugs, medications can help us manage physical withdrawal symptoms and allow us to focus on managing external and other internal triggers. Medications may also be necessary for a safe medical detox.

- For some addictions, like those to alcohol and drugs, residential programs can help provide a temporary situation where we no longer have easy access to these substances, and a chance to learn how to manage cravings more effectively.

- We can meet other people who encounter similar challenges with managing cravings, and we can inspire and motivate each other.

- Addiction professionals can also help us to work on our relapse prevention plans and check in with us to make sure we are on the right track.

The professional help options include psychotherapy, medication, detoxification and rehabilitation programs, and self-help groups. Treatment needs to be tailored to each individual and situation, and a combination of treatment approaches can also be helpful. Treatment options should address the types of addictive behaviors we are engaging in, how long we have been managing cravings and addictions, how severe the addiction is, and how our cravings and addictive behaviors are impacting our lives.

Counseling or psychotherapy is an important source of support for many people who are managing cravings. These treatments can be delivered individually or in a group format. Couples or family therapy can also be helpful to work out any issues that involve partners or family members. Treatments can focus on helping us increase our motivation to manage our cravings, learn how to more effectively deal with them, and sustain progress once we have made significant positive changes in our lives.

Medication can be helpful for managing cravings for smoking, drinking, and using drugs. Many smoking-cessation medications are available over the counter, including nicotine patches, nicotine lozenges, and nicotine gum. Others are available by prescription. These medications can help ease nicotine withdrawal symptoms and, again, help us to better focus on other internal and external triggers for smoking. Medications are also often part of effective treatment for moderate to severe addictions to drugs and alcohol. These medications can also ease withdrawal symptoms from substances, help reduce cravings, and prevent relapse. However, medications for drugs and alcohol are not usually used on their own and should be combined with psychotherapy or engagement in addiction programs.

For more serious addictions, detoxification is necessary. This helps limit withdrawal symptoms while the body clears itself of the substance. Before attempting to try to detox on your own (which in some cases can be dangerous), it is essential to discuss with a provider whether this process could benefit you. In addition, for addiction to drugs and alcohol, longer-term rehabilitation programs can also help you remain abstinent from drugs and alcohol and focus on improving important aspects of your life.

Self-help or support groups can also be a key source of support for managing cravings. These groups are composed of people who are also experiencing similar challenges with managing cravings. Participating in these groups can help us to feel more supported and less alone on our journey to managing cravings. It can be very satisfying to share your story and help others with their challenges. Many groups are available to help people manage cravings for food, tobacco, alcohol, and drugs.

Those trying to manage cravings and stop using substances often have tried many different approaches with no success, so they're understandably hesitant to seek out new sources of support. Whether we seek out these sources of support depends on our situation and motivation. Seeking them out, when warranted or necessary, can help provide support for managing cravings more effectively and help us head in the direction of our values.

Choice Moment Aids

Establishing a helpful social support network can be paramount to our success in managing cravings and addictive behaviors. We discussed how to recognize helpful and unhelpful support, how to seek out sources of helpful support, and how to respond to and manage those that aren't helpful. We presented effective communication skills and recommendations as to when it may be important to seek professional help. The obstacles and skills embedded in this chapter are summarized in the following figure. Remember to add the obstacles and skills you learned in this chapter to your own Craving Choice Moment Diagram from the online free tools.

Toward My Values

Craving Choice Moment

Aids (Skills)
- Identify helpful sources of support.
- Build a helpful social support network.
- Use effective communication skills.
- Deal with unhelpful support:
  * Leave.
  * Change what you can.
  * Accept what you cannot change, and act based on values.
- Seek professional help.

Away from My Values

Obstacles
Unhelpful social support

Bringing It All Together

- Helpful, supportive social support is vital to managing cravings. Our social support network can talk us through challenging cravings and help us feel less alone on our path to a healthier life. Our supports can help encourage us to focus on our values and reach our goals.

- If we don't have helpful sources of support in our lives, it is important to seek new sources of support. Being willing to meet new people, listen, be open and honest with them, use effective communication skills, and provide support in return all can help new relationships to develop and thrive.

- We need to be careful about having unhelpful supports in our life, as these can potentially undermine our progress in managing cravings and making positive life choices.

- It can be helpful, and sometimes necessary, to seek out professional help to manage long-standing and impairing addictions. We
encourage you to not hesitate (no matter what your mind may be
saying) to seek out professional help for managing cravings and
addictions.

Bringing Our Learning to Life

What is one step that you can take this week to develop better supports for
managing cravings in your life? Take that one step and see the difference
it makes for you.

We are nearing the end of our work together in managing cravings. In
the next chapter, we will focus on how to sustain all the progress you have
made.

CHAPTER 13

Managing Cravings for the Long Run

Jeff *I am so glad and thankful I got to try this approach. I could never imagine that struggling with my thoughts, feelings, and cravings was the problem. I gained a whole new perspective on life. I now know what matters to me and where I want my life to go. I can set goals, I am able to recognize obstacles when they appear, and I willingly focus on my actions. I recognize what I can and cannot control. I also recognize that the cravings and all the things I feel and think do not determine who I am. I am comfortable with who I am, and I can be compassionate toward myself and others. I do sometimes fall into autopilot mode, yet I am able to return to the present and redirect my actions. I have new relationships and hobbies that I care about, and I feel free, liberated, and whole.*

Let us take a moment to congratulate you. You have come a long way, and you should be proud of that. Congratulations on getting this far! We hope this will be the beginning of a new way of living for you.

Hoping Your Journey Is Long

When we start on our values-based living journey, we need to continuously choose to behave in accordance with what we care about, if we care to stay on our chosen path. One of Maria's favorite poets, Constantine Cavafis, wrote a poem called "Ithaka" which beautifully speaks to this idea. We highly recommend reading the poem or listening to a recorded version online. As Cavafis's poem suggests, the experiences we gain along the way to living in accordance with our values are what really matter, not necessarily reaching a final destination. This is the approach we encourage you to take in life: savoring every moment along the way on your valued life journey.

When we start on our values-based living journey, we need to continuously choose to behave in accordance with what we care about, if we care to stay on our chosen path. As Cavafis's poem suggests, the experiences we gain along the way to living in accordance with our values are what really matter, not necessarily reaching a final destination. This is the approach we encourage you to take in life: savoring every moment along the way on your valued life journey.

Runners usually say that they need to run two to three kilometers before they start to feel the sensations of joy and exhilaration flowing through their bodies. This suggests that they have to pull through the initial two to three difficult kilometers of discomfort and body challenge before they start to enjoy the benefits. This is different from the immediate reinforcement we may get by eating a chocolate, having a drink, or smoking, for which we do not have to work hard or wait. Usually, the most important and valuable things in life take time and persistence to achieve. Persistence involves continuing our efforts, as a choice, in the face of obstacles. Choosing to continue when our minds start to play their games, telling us to quit or give up. Persisting because we care about our valued domains and how we want to live our lives.

Let's exercise our persistence muscle together. Practice persisting as an act when discomfort shows up. You can record this yourself or download the audio file from the online free tools at http://www.newharbinger.com/48336.

EXERCISE: Staying Still

Find a place to sit or lie down where you will not be disturbed for the new few minutes. Close your eyes or find a spot to gently gaze at. Bring your attention to your body, recognizing that it is continuously sensing the environment around you. Bring your attention to your breath and notice any sensations you may have as you breathe in and out. When thoughts divert your attention, take a moment to notice where these thoughts have taken you without judging them, and come back to your breath, making room within you for these thoughts. Remember to come back to your breath each time your mind wanders.

Now return your attention to your body. Start with your toes and move up, slowly scanning every part of your body till you reach the top of your head. Notice the way you are sitting or lying and how your body weight gently presses what supports you. As you pay attention to your body, practice staying completely still. Nothing moves, except from the breathing action of your chest. You may notice feeling itchy somewhere or a desire to move a part of your body. You may feel some discomfort somewhere. Just notice these desires or discomforts without trying to fulfill or change them in any way. Just stay still. Notice your body, your sensations, your thoughts that may be asking you to act in some way. Notice also that you are staying completely still, even if these requests are present. Continue to stay still as you observe these sensations within your body without responding to them. Watch them with curiosity as if you have never experienced them before. Watch them come and watch them go. You do not need to feel or think anything specific, just stay still. Continue to observe as you stay still for a few more moments. If something distracts you, notice it, allow it to be there, and return to paying attention while staying still.

When you are ready, slowly return your attention to the room around you and the sounds inside and outside the room, and open your eyes.

How was this experience?

Many individuals at first find it impossible to stay still or not respond to whatever their mind is telling them to do—to scratch an itch on their face, or move their hand, and so on. Yet if you persist in your noticing, without satisfying the mind's requests, you will discover that these sensations indeed come and go, and you will be able to stay still. Remember, the same thing applies when it comes to cravings—they come and they go, just like waves in the sea.

Bringing All of Our Learning Together

We hope that by now you have gained lots of skills and new tools for your life's toolbox. Now we would like you to put all your skills together in order to be able to recognize signs that you are on your valued-living path or starting to veer off so you can redirect yourself.

EXERCISE: Writing Your New Values-Based Living Story
(inspired by Lillis et al., 2014)

In this exercise we invite you to consider all that you have learned in this book and use it to write your New Values-Based Living Story. This is your story and you are its hero—its main character. As with any good story plot, the hero will face challenges and difficulties. Give your hero a name. It can be your name or one you choose that has some meaning for you. Fai, for example, named her hero Savorita as a tribute to choosing to savor life. You can also give your story a title. Kap, for example, titled his story *Breathing Life*, which he explained was a reminder of his new smoke-free life: *breathing life rather than smog*. Amy named hers *Finding Amy*, as she wanted the story to be about her finding herself and her valued path in life. Be as creative as you want here and choose what fits your experiences. If it is hard to find your title from the beginning, it's okay. Proceed with your story; the title may jump out later.

As with many good stories, this one has several sections.

SECTION 1: *New Beginnings*

In this section the hero chooses to make a new beginning, which starts with values. As we've discussed, values are our internal compass, the lighthouse that helps us find our way; they can help us find the new direction in which we would like to head in. We recommend you now draw your valued-living path (the figure on the following page presents Fai's example) on the blank path map found with the online free tools.

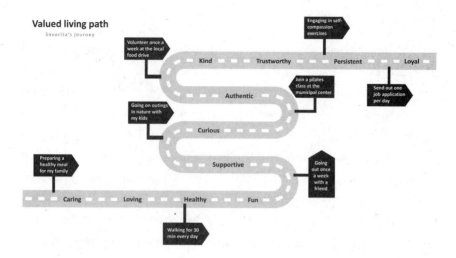

Valued living path
Savorita's journey

Engaging in self-compassion exercises

Volunteer once a week at the local food drive

Kind   Trustworthy   Persistent   Loyal

Join a pilates class at the municipal center

Authentic

Send out one job application per day

Going on outings in nature with my kids

Curious

Preparing a healthy meal for my family

Supportive

Going out once a week with a friend

Caring   Loving   Healthy   Fun

Walking for 30 min every day

Along the path, write down some of the values you have previously identified, so that you remember the direction you chose for your path to values-based living. Add signs to help you know when you are heading in the right direction. These signs are the goals you've identified for yourself in previous chapters. If you prefer, you can have different valued paths for different life domains (say, one for family, another for friendship, health, or work) and add more signs/goals along the way for that valued domain (for health you might add goals like "cooking at least one healthy meal per day," "going to a dancing class once a week," or "sleeping at least six hours each night"). Adapt this exercise to suit your needs and what will help you the most; experiment and find what works for you. Just because something worked for someone else does not mean it will work the same way for you, so adapt it to fit your needs.

When you look at this map, we want you to be able to immediately recognize whether you are on your valued-living path. If you realize that you may have veered off the path, use this choice moment to regroup. Go through the STOP points you learned in chapter 11 and choose to get back to your valued-living path and the story you want to be living.

SECTION 2: *Conflict*

As with any good adventure story, you are bound to run into difficulties and saboteurs along the way. These will try to get you off course by telling you to do things inconsistent with your values-based living. Most of these saboteurs are familiar to you, as they have been with you for most of your life. These are your unwanted thoughts, feelings, sensations, and cravings. They are Mr. "I am too weak," Miss "I am a failure," Madam "This is too much, too hard," Dr. "One drink/smoke/sweet won't matter," Mrs. "I cannot stand this feeling," Captain "My heart is beating too fast," and the Indulgence Monster.

Find your saboteurs and give them names. Search for at least five saboteurs, making sure that you have at least one to represent thoughts, feelings, sensations, memories, cravings, and incorporate them into your story. Give them a personality and a past. Fai named one of her saboteurs "Choc the Craving Stud," a smooth, smartly dressed, good-looking fellow who has a way with words, is charming and convincing. He chooses to show up when Savorita is at her most vulnerable points. One of Fai's other saboteurs was the "Cannot Menace," a troublemaker kid (like Dennis the Menace) who follows Savorita around creating all sorts of traps for her, making it easy for her to fail. Her third saboteur was the "Hunger Giant," a tall, chubby, somewhat cute grandmotherly giant who constantly brings up sensations and cues of hunger and encourages Savorita to eat. We're encouraging you to be playful with these saboteurs, which research suggests helps change your perspective to better manage them.

Who are your saboteurs? You can go back and review previous chapters to help you identify all those thoughts, sensations, and cravings that tend to show up for you. Then describe how they act and what they tell you.

Next, write a few lines about how the hero used to react to these saboteurs. How did the hero deal with the saboteurs? If they tried to fight with the saboteurs, what happened? How did the fight end? Did the hero end up trying to appease the saboteurs, give up or give in? Search for avoidance moves where the hero opted for short-term relief at the expense of long-term values-based living. How did the hero's behavior impact their life path? Explore how the hero may have been continuously falling off the path or even following paths other than the chosen valued-living one.

While you are writing this, contemplate whether these saboteurs were really out to get the hero. Is Choc the Craving Stud really out to hurt Savorita? Is the Cannot Menace evil and out to get her? Is the Hunger Giant trying to harm the hero? Or are these seeming saboteurs—these thoughts, feelings, sensations—really well meaning and somehow trying to help or protect the hero, even if they're somewhat misguided? Maybe Choc wants to please our hero, provide support and help our hero feel better or cope using the only method he knows. Maybe the grandmotherly Hunger Giant is just trying to make sure that Savorita is well fed because she does not want her to go hungry. Or the Cannot Menace reminds her of past times when she failed, attempting to motivate her for future actions; he wants her to be her best self and worries about her.

These saboteurs may actually have good intentions. The problem is, when we change our life they cannot keep up. When we are trying to live a healthy life, it's counterproductive to listen to misguided sensations of needing to use, drink, or smoke. To just appease the saboteurs leaves us empty. It's as if you want to hang a new picture on your wall, and instead of a hammer your mind hands you a fishing rod. A fishing rod is a great and useful tool—for fishing! But it will not help you hang a picture on the wall. Same with the saboteurs. They mean well, yet the tools they provide are not the ones you need to stay on your valued-living path. In your story, explore the intentions of your saboteurs, noticing that these intentions may be good yet are misguided for the purpose at hand.

SECTION 3: *Perseverance*

As the story progresses, the hero recognizes the saboteurs' intentions as benevolent yet misguided. With this knowledge, our hero can stop fighting with the saboteurs and change the way they interact with them. Our hero can even extend some kindness, compassion, and acknowledgment to these saboteurs. The hero can allow the saboteurs to accompany them on their valued-living journey. It is like the hero is taking along a radio. At times this radio may be a nice companion, playing the music our hero enjoys listening to; at others, this radio may broadcast annoying advertisements or music that the hero is not particularly fond of. The key here is that our hero can *choose* whether to continue their journey, taking along this radio (the saboteurs), with whatever it broadcasts, along for the ride.

Consider your five saboteurs and write about how the hero can now interact with each of them. Write about how the hero can now respond to them with kindness, compassion, and care. Review all the skills learned in this book and use them to change the way you relate to the saboteurs while progressing on your own valued-living journey. When you run into someone like the Craving Stud, instead of trying to exorcize him, you can recognize he simply doesn't know better—this is the only way he knows how to cope. And you can bring him along with you while learning and practicing your new coping skills. If a saboteur like the Cannot Menace shows up, recognize that he has good intentions and is trying to help motivate you. Show him that your values are your motivators now, and embark together on your new life adventures. Write about how our hero demonstrates kindness toward each saboteur and invites them along.

The hero may even discover that though the saboteurs looked really scary at the beginning, they may no longer seem so now. Recall the story of the *Wizard of Oz*, in which Dorothy was initially scared of the Lion, the Scarecrow, and the Tin Man, yet she invited each one along for the journey to find the Wizard of Oz. Dorothy became friends with and even grew fond of these companions. Yes, they could be annoying at times or cause some trouble, but they meant well and were actually helping her to reach her goals. Remember, when the saboteurs show up, it is a chance for you to practice your skills and grow. Write how the hero will behave when the saboteurs show up in different high-risk situations. You may have been doing well in quitting your habits of smoking, drinking, using drugs, or eating unhealthily; then one day your boss invites you to a party at his house and you have to attend. There you encounter all the cues that would trigger using, smoking, or overeating in the past. The Craving Stud shows up in all his glory, ready to lure you into the old way of behaving. Even if the Craving Stud wants you to enjoy something that he knows you like, you can compassionately acknowledge his efforts, let him try his charms, and choose the way you want to behave, remembering your valued-living path.

SECTION 4: *Living Life*

Sometimes the hero may realize they've veered off course. Lapses can happen, as we've discussed. Write about how the hero will manage these based on lessons from the previous chapters. Remember, approaching the saboteurs with kindness and self-compassion reflects the qualities of a real hero.

Developing Your Long-Term Goal Game Plan

This book is only the beginning of your journey—there is much road ahead of you! It can be helpful to think about what you want to keep accomplishing on the road to a healthier life. Think about your long-term goal game plan. It can help to list the goals you still want to accomplish and any barriers that may come up. With the online free tools (http://www .newharbinger.com/48336), we included sample worksheets where you can continue to fill out your values, goals, strategies to accomplish these goals, and strategies to overcome any barriers that arise. Keep using these worksheets to help you with committed action in the long term. The more you live up to what is important to you, the more likely you are to manage cravings better in the long term, and the more satisfied you are likely to be.

Choice Moment Aids

Throughout the book we've pointed out obstacles and barriers to values-based living and identified sources that can place you at risk for choosing self-defeating behaviors that take you away from the things you care about and how you want your life to unfold. For each obstacle, we proposed new skills for choosing life-enhancing behaviors that will take you toward living your values and a vital, vibrant life. The Craving Choice Moment Diagram shown here summarizes these. Print out your own version from the online free tools and note all your personal obstacles and favorite skills. We hope this will be a powerful tool to always have with you.

Toward My Values

Craving Choice Moment

Away from My Values

Aids (Skills)

- Managing external and intern triggers
- Acting with willingness
- Facing cravings
- Identifying values
- Cognitive defusion
- Knowing you are more than your cravings
- Being in the present moment (mindfulness)
- Self-compassion
- Values-based goals
- ACT
  * Accept your reactions and be present
  * Choose a valued direction
  * Take action
- Managing slips and relapses
- STOP
  * Slow down
  * Take note
  * Open up
  * Pursue valued actions
- Identifying helpful sources of support
- Building a helpful social support network
- Using communication skills
- Dealing with unhelpful support
  * Leave
  * Change what you can
  * Accept what you cannot change and act based on values
- Seeking professional help

Obstacles

- Tactics to control cravings
- Stories we make about ourselves
- Believing in the illusions our mind produces.
- Going into autopilot mode
- Stigma and shame
- FEAR
  * Fusion with thoughts
  * Evaluation of experience
  * Avoidance
  * Reason-giving
- Challenges to managing cravings
- Unhelpful social support

Life Happens

We wrote this book to help you live the most vital life possible based on what matters to you. We wanted to help you decrease your suffering and improve your quality of life for the long run. We hope you have started to apply the skills learned in this book and begun to see the benefits. Values-based living requires perseverance, effort, practice, and willingness to behave in accordance with what matters to us, even when it is hard or we do not want to. Life happens, and all we can do is choose how we want to live it. It really all comes down to one choice, what we call the willingness question: Are you willing to choose to live based on your values, even when it is hard or uncomfortable, or your mind is giving you reasons not to, or cravings show up? In each situation you have this choice, even if it does not seem obvious. You always have a choice for how you behave—what you say and what you do, *not* what you think or how you feel. Life will continue to unspool, with all its glory and its mess, no matter what. How do you choose to act and live? We hope you will choose to live a vital, rich, and meaningful life.

Congratulations on completing this book! And remember, you can return to it (as well as the online free tools) again and again, revisiting and reinforcing what is most helpful and effective for you.

Conclusion

In this book, we have followed the paths of several people who had difficulty managing cravings and who tried the skills discussed here. These were real individuals we have worked with over the years; to preserve confidentiality, we changed some of the information. To wrap up, let's check back in with them and see how the use of these skills transformed their approach to managing cravings and changed their lives for the better.

Amy

Amy is enjoying healthy living. She learned to manage her life better, and as a result her anxiety is much reduced. She of course still gets pretty stressed at times, especially by problems at work, and this brings up cravings for junk food. She particularly loves to use the STOP technique; it helps redirect her attention to her values of healthy living, and most of the time she chooses to not indulge in junk food. When she has it every now and then, it's usually a conscious choice not based on cravings.

Kap

Kap quit smoking and was smoke-free for three months. Then his brother died, and while grieving he ended up smoking again. He realized that after his brother's death he'd stopped using the skills he'd learned, so he reached out for help again. He was able to reconnect with his values, and by practicing his cognitive defusion skills and mindful awareness of cravings and obstacles to quitting, he was able to quit again. He has now been smoke-free for two years. He calls Maria every year in October on the anniversary of his quit date. He reports that the cravings have almost completely disappeared. A small "reminiscent craving" (as he calls it) shows up from time to time when he meets with his smoking buddies or goes to a bar or a club where people are smoking, yet he reminds himself of his journey to date and is able to turn to his action plan and not smoke.

Fai

It has been three years since Fai started to use the skills outlined in this book to change her approach to managing cravings and her life. She reports that she has been able to get a job that she likes. This helped with her being able to engage in other activities she enjoys, such as dance classes and traveling. She continues to describe herself as a chocolate lover, yet she now says that she is so much more than that. She also describes herself as an international food connoisseur. She loves traveling and tasting new foods and chocolates from all around the world. She reports that her relationship with her cravings, thoughts, and feelings has changed. It is not a dependency or a struggling relationship any more. Fai says she frequently practices mindfulness and acceptance and cognitive defusion exercises, which help remind her that she can make room for all these internal experiences and choose to act based on values. She stated, "I am finally living my valued life. It is not always easy, but it is definitely more satisfying."

Jeff

Jeff has now been clean of drug use and other addictive behaviors for about two years. Following our treatment, he has been able to move on with his life. He is now married, and he and his wife are expecting their first baby. He has a group of really helpful, supportive friends. Jeff also has a job he enjoys; he feels like he belongs and is contributing significantly to society. He says there are "dark" days, yet knowing that each moment is a choice moment, and that he can always choose something different, gives him freedom. This enables him to choose to move toward his valued-living path each time. He tries to engage in at least one valued-living action every day and continues to make notes in his notebook to remind himself to use his skills and of how far he has come.

Alex

Alex is doing very well. He was able to forgive himself for his past actions and his drinking. He was also able to utilize his communication and relationship skills to rebuild his relationship with his sister, who has been an immense source of support for him on his sobriety journey. Alex is now in a relationship and hopes to soon start his own family. He holds a steady job, and for the first time he reports feeling truly "human." There are bad days when the cravings get hard to manage or when he passes by a bar or meets up with a drinking buddy, yet he uses all his skills to manage these cravings. He says he is on alert, as he knows he does not want to go back; instead, he uses his therapy tools and his values compass to move forward.

We wish you the best in your own journey!

Acknowledgments

We are very grateful to New Harbinger and the whole team there, particularly Elizabeth Hollis Hansen and Clancy Drake, for giving us a chance to put our thoughts and our workings into a book, providing editing, and guiding us through the process of development and publication.

Maria: My biggest thanks and gratitude to Dr. Steven Hayes, for all his wisdom and support; his ideas and innovations have influenced my life and career path. Big thanks to the other developers of the acceptance and commitment therapy (ACT) approach, Kelly Wilson and Kirk Strosahl—your ideas and contributions are the foundation we build on. Many thanks to Russ Harris for ingeniously turning ideas and theoretical concepts into simple language and material he openly shares, and for supporting this book. Thanks also to amazing collaborators I have worked with through the years, particularly JoAnne Dahl and Andrew Gloster for their endless support. Big thanks to the Association for Contextual Behavioral Science community for the knowledge, support, sharing of ideas, conversations, and opportunities. I am very grateful to have an amazing group of students, graduates, and researchers enriching my ACThealthy laboratory community; they are always supportive of my ideas and projects. I am blessed to have such smart, talented individuals surround me. Finally, a big thanks to my family, who inspire me to create and allow me the space to do so.

Megan: My thanks to my mentors who influenced my intervention development and clinical work over the years, including Drs. Katharine Phillips, Douglas Ziedonis, David Kalman, and Judith Cooney. I extend gratitude to my collaborators, particularly Drs. Erin Reilly, Jaimee Heffner, Victoria Ameral, and Steven Shirk. I am forever grateful to my family, who have supported me during my long nights of writing this book. I am also grateful to the many people I have served over the years as a clinician—you all have provided tremendous meaning in my life and give me a reason to keep innovating in my clinical practice.

References

Biglan, A., Hayes, S. C., & Pistorello, J. (2008). Acceptance and commitment: Implications for prevention science. *Prevention Science, 9*(3), 139–152.

Carmichael, C. L., Reis, H. T., & Duberstein, P. R. (2015). In your 20s it's quantity, in your 30s it's quality: The prognostic value of social activity across 30 years of adulthood. *Psychology and Aging, 30,* 95–105. doi:10.1037/pag0000014.

Cavafis, K. P. (1911). Ithaka. In *The complete poems of Cavafy* (exp. ed.). New York, NY: Harcourt.

Centers for Disease Control. (2020). Excessive alcohol use. Washington, DC: CDC. https://www.cdc.gov/chronicdisease/pdf/factsheets/alcohol -use-factsheet-H.pdf

Chikritzhs, T. N., Jonas, H. A., Stockwell, T. R., Heale, P. F., & Dietze, P. M. (2001). Mortality and life-years lost to alcohol: A comparison of acute and chronic cases. *Medical Journal of Australia, 174,* 281–284.

Gendall, K. A., Joyce, P. R., & Sullivan, P. F. (1997). Impact of definition on prevalence of food cravings in a random sample of young women. *Appetite, 28,* 63–72. doi:10.1006/appe.1996.0060.

Gloster, A. T., Walder, N., Levin, M. E., Twohig, M. P., & Karekla, M. (2020). The empirical status of acceptance and commitment therapy: A review of meta-analyses. *Journal of Contextual Behavior Science, 18,* 181–192. https://doi.org/10.1016/j.jcbs.2020.09.009.

Harris, R. (2009). *ACT made simple: A quick-start guide to ACT basics and beyond.* Oakland, CA: New Harbinger.

Harris, R. (2019). *ACT made simple: An easy-to-read primer on acceptance and commitment therapy.* Oakland, CA: New Harbinger.

Hayes, L. L., & Ciarrochi, J. (2015). *The thriving adolescent: Using acceptance and commitment therapy and positive psychology to help teens manage emotions, achieve goals, and build connection.* Oakland, CA: New Harbinger.

Hayes, S. C. (2005). *Get out of your mind and into your life: The new ACT.* Oakland, CA: New Harbinger.

Hayes, S. C., Strosahl, K. D., & Wilson, K. G. (1999). *Acceptance and commitment therapy: An experiential approach to behavior change.* New York, NY: Guilford Press.

Hill, A. J. (2007). The psychology of food craving. *Proceedings of the Nutrition Society, 66,* 277–285. doi:10.1017/S0029665107005502.

Jha, P., Ramasundararahettige, C., Landsman, V., Rostran, B., Thun, M., Anderson, R. N. et al. (2013). 21st-century hazards of smoking and benefits of cessation in the United States. *New England Journal of Medicine, 368,* 341–350. doi:10.1056/NEJMsa1211128.

Kabat-Zinn, J. (2016). Sitting meditations. *Mindfulness, 7*(6), 1441–1444.

Karekla, M. (2010). ACT-based smoking cessation for adolescents and young adults: Group therapy protocol. Unpublished protocol.

Killingsworth, M. A., & Gilbert, D. T. (2010). A wandering mind is an unhappy mind. *Science, 330*(6006), 932.

Lillis, J., Dahl, J., & Weineland, S. M. (2014). *The diet trap: Feed your psychological needs and end the weight loss struggle using acceptance and commitment therapy.* Oakland, CA: New Harbinger.

Lung, T., Jan, S., Tan, E. J., Killedar, A., & Hayes, A. (2019). Impact of overweight, obesity, and severe obesity on life expectancy of Australian adults. *International Journal of Obesity, 43,* 782–789. doi:10.1038/s41366-018-0210-2.

Luoma, J. B., & Kohlenberg, B. S. (2012). Self-stigma and shame in addictions. In S. C. Hayes & M. E. Levin (Eds.), *Mindfulness and acceptance for addictive behaviors.* Oakland, CA: New Harbinger.

Neff, K. (2003). Self-compassion: An alternative conceptualization of a healthy attitude toward oneself. *Self and identity, 2*(2), 85-101.

Nikolaou, P., & Karekla, M. (2017). ACT to prevent eating disorders: Evaluation of the AcceptME digital gamified prevention program based on acceptance and commitment therapy. Dissertation, University of Cyprus. Unpublished protocol.

Smyth, B., Hoffman, V., Fan, J., & Hser, Y. (2007). Years of potential life lost among heroin addicts 33 years after treatment. *Preventive Medicine, 44,* 369–374. doi:10.1016/j.ypmed.2006.10.003.

Taylor, S. E. (2011). *Social support: A review.* In H. S. Friedman (Ed.), *Oxford library of psychology: The Oxford handbook of health psychology* (pp. 189–214). Oxford, UK: Oxford University Press. doi:10.1093/oxfordhb/9780195342819.013.0009.

Vowles, K. E., & McCracken, L. M. (2010). Comparing the role of psychological flexibility and traditional pain management coping strategies in chronic pain treatment outcomes. *Behaviour Research and Therapy, 48*(2), 141–146.

Maria Karekla, PhD, is a licensed clinical psychologist, and associate professor at the University of Cyprus where she heads the ACT*healthy* Clinical Psychology and Behavioral Medicine laboratory. She is a peer-reviewed acceptance and commitment therapy (ACT) therapy trainer, and presently serves as the president-elect of the Association for Contextual Behavioral Science (ACBS) where she has been a fellow since 2019. She is also a fellow of the Society of Behavioral Medicine (SBM). She was nominated in 2017 for the National Literary Awards in the children/adolescents category, and also for her illustrations for the book. She has received numerous national and international awards and grants for her research work. In 2018, she was nominated as Cyprus Woman of the Year in the academic/researcher category.

Megan M. Kelly, PhD, is a licensed clinical psychologist, and associate professor in the department of psychiatry at the University of Massachusetts Medical School. She has been involved in addictions research for the past sixteen years, with a particular focus on the development of behavioral interventions for individuals with comorbid addictions and mental health disorders. She has received several VA- and NIH-funded awards to develop and evaluate new behavioral interventions and programs for individuals with co-occurring disorders using ACT principles. She has evaluated, treated, or supervised the treatment of over 2,000 people struggling with addictions.

Foreword author **Russ Harris** is an internationally acclaimed acceptance and commitment therapy (ACT) trainer, and author of the best-selling ACT-based self-help book, *The Happiness Trap*, which has sold more than one million copies and been published in thirty languages. He is widely renowned for his ability to teach ACT in a way that is simple, clear, and fun—yet extremely practical.

ABOUT US

Founded by psychologist Matthew McKay and Patrick Fanning, New Harbinger has published books that promote wellness in mind, body, and spirit for more than forty-five years.

Our proven-effective self-help books and pioneering workbooks help readers of all ages and backgrounds make positive lifestyle changes, improve mental health and well-being, and achieve meaningful personal growth. In addition, our spirituality books offer profound guidance for deepening awareness and cultivating healing, self-discovery, and fulfillment.

New Harbinger is proud to be an independent and employee-owned company, publishing books that reflect its core values of integrity, innovation, commitment, sustainability, compassion, and trust. Written by leaders in the field and recommended by therapists worldwide, New Harbinger books are practical, reliable, and provide real tools for real change.

newharbingerpublications

FROM OUR PUBLISHER—

As the publisher at New Harbinger and a clinical psychologist since 1978, I know that emotional problems are best helped with evidence-based therapies. These are the treatments derived from scientific research (randomized controlled trials) that show what works. Whether these treatments are delivered by trained clinicians or found in a self-help book, they are designed to provide you with proven strategies to overcome your problem.

Therapies that aren't evidence-based—whether offered by clinicians or in books—are much less likely to help. In fact, therapies that aren't guided by science may not help you at all. That's why this New Harbinger book is based on scientific evidence that the treatment can relieve emotional pain.

This is important: if this book isn't enough, and you need the help of a skilled therapist, use the following resources to find a clinician trained in the evidence-based protocols appropriate for your problem. And if you need more support—a community that understands what you're going through and can show you ways to cope—resources for that are provided below, as well.

Real help is available for the problems you have been struggling with. The skills you can learn from evidence-based therapies will change your life.

Matthew McKay, PhD
Publisher, New Harbinger Publications

If you need a therapist, the following organization can help you find a therapist trained in acceptance and commitment therapy (ACT).

Association for Contextual Behavioral Science (ACBS)
please visit www.contextualscience.org and click on *Find an ACT Therapist*.

For additional support for patients, family, and friends, please contact the following:

Anxiety and Depression Association of American (ADAA)
please visit www.adaa.org

National Center for PTSD
visit www.ptsd.va.gov

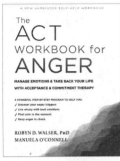

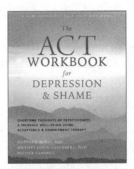

Did you know there are **free tools** you can download for this book?

Free tools are things like **worksheets, guided meditation exercises**, and **more** that will help you get the most out of your book.

You can download free tools for this book—whether you bought or borrowed it, in any format, from any source—from the New Harbinger website. All you need is a NewHarbinger.com account. Just use the URL provided in this book to view the free tools that are available for it. Then, click on the "download" button for the free tool you want, and follow the prompts that appear to log in to your NewHarbinger.com account and download the material.

You can also save the free tools for this book to your **Free Tools Library** so you can access them again anytime, just by logging in to your account! Just look for this button on the book's free tools page.

+ Save this to my free tools library

If you need help accessing or downloading free tools, visit **newharbinger.com/faq** or contact us at **customerservice@newharbinger.com**.